NIÑEZ
Spanish Songs, Games and Stories of Childhood

Virginia Nylander Ebinger

SUNSTONE PRESS

SANTA FE
New Mexico

Cover Illustration by Sue Rolston Blackburn

Printed in the United States of America

10 9 8 7 6 5 4 3 2

Library of Congress Cataloging in Publication Data:
  Niñez: Spanish songs, games, and stories of childhood/Virginia Nylander Ebinger.—1st ed.
    p.cm.
  English and Spanish.
  "The area of concentration is New MExico and southern Colorado"—p.5
  ISBN: 0-86534-175-3; $8.95
  1. Games—Southwest, New—Folklore. 2.Amusements—Southwest, New—Forklore. 3. Folk songs, Spanish—Southwest, Nw. 4. Children's stories, Spanish American—Southwest, Nw.
I. Title. II. Title: Spanish songs, games, and stories of childhood.
GR 108.5.E25   1993   93-3215
398'.0979+dc20   CIP

Published by SUNSTONE PRESS
              Post Office Box 2321
              Santa Fe, NM 87504-2321 / USA
              (505) 988-4418 / *orders only* (800) 243-5644
              FAX (505) 988-1025

CONTENTS

PREFACE

A lo escrito has de agarrarte...que las palabras...se las lleva el aire.[1]
You must write it down...the air carries away your words.

This book is a celebration of survival.

I have collected Spanish folk materials almost all my life, at first not deliberately, hardly realizing I was doing it until the past few years. I have become, now, an active and fully aware collector because along with the collecting I have grown to appreciate the difficulties this folk culture has had to overcome and, especially, the forces it still must face, again and again, in order to continue to survive. I hope this book will help.

It concentrates on children's folklore for at least two reasons. First, my professional life has been devoted to teaching children and, more recently, to teaching teachers of children. This has been, therefore, the area of greatest interest to me. The second reason is more important: Unless the *children* know, survival of a culture will not—cannot—continue to be an option. It becomes harder and harder—amidst the noises of the outside, the calls for attention by countless other agents, the good/bad efforts to "mainstream" or to add to "the melting pot"—to keep alive a cultural history and to find necessary means to transmit it to the children. And so I hope this collection will be one such means. I hope it will awaken memories and long-past images for some readers; I hope it will create a new interest and appreciation for others; and I especially hope it will be a pleasurable source of learning for the children.

A few things need to be explained. Although some of the material is found in Mexico and other areas of the Spanish-speaking Americas, and much of it is spread among Spanish-speaking areas of the United States, the area of concentration is New Mexico and southern Colorado. It is here that the Spanish roots are most apparent, and it is these roots and the fruit that has come from nurturing them that form the basis for these materials. The title, *Ninez*, means childhood.

Then there's the language. I have heard wise people talk about how to destroy a culture: Start by taking away its language. Not too many years ago, Spanish speaking was looked on, to say the least, with disfavor. A result of that is a generation or two of people of Spanish heritage who barely know the language. These attitudes, happily, are changing, and Spanish is once again spoken with pride. You will find in this book translations sufficient for understanding the meaning of the words—unless they are simply the nonsense words found in children's play materials in all cultures—but no "singable translations." These songs and rhymes and game formulas are meant to be re-created in the language in which they arose. The rhythms, the rhymes and assonances, and even some of the magic are gone, or at the very least compromised, once translation sets in.

The gender question is always difficult in writing. *He/she, s/he, him/her,* and other such awkward ways of writing or speaking of one person of either sex seem to be inefficient and clumsy. I have, therefore, with apologies to those whom it offends, almost always used *he* or *him*.

I have so many people to thank: those who have given me direct help by sharing their memories or leading me to others who would; many writers who have trod some of these same paths before me; collectors and reporters, some of them anonymous, who were responsible for creating the WPA files in the 30's and 40's—still a wealth of barely touched folk treasures; students I have taught over many years; friends who have inspired or encouraged, sometimes without their even knowing it; friends who have helped with difficult translation problems; and my family: daughter Mary who went with me to Spain—even unto the Biblioteca Nacional—in search of roots; daughter Anne who married a descendant of early New Mexicans and with him produced two little "coyotes," Mary Victoria and Philip Santiago, who will forever be proud of their heritage; to sons Michael (along with Laura and Carl) and John on general principles; and to husband Gene who has gone along with it all, almost always with good spirit.

INTRODUCTION

El bien no es conocido hasta que es perdido.[2]
The good is not appreciated until it is lost.

The history of the Iberian peninsula leaves little doubt as to the *de facto* mixture, and thus the richness, of cultures within its borders. Phoenician seamen, Carthaginian empire builders, Greek traders—all came in pre-Christian times to this geographically sensitive land abutted by the sea on three sides, within sight of northern Africa, attached by an enormous mountain range to the large land mass of Europe; fertile; filled with possibilities for building defenses. Here they found pastoral peoples, descendants of some of the oldest known civilizations on earth—Celts, Vascones, Astures.

Spain was a prize to be seized by the Roman colonizers, and in turn it was ripe for Christianization. The Visigoths came, the Franks, the Vandals, and Jews from Africa and the Middle East. Through the ages North Africans had made their way across the narrow strait to Spain, but the early eighth century brought full-scale invasion and conquest by the Moslems which was to last, at least in some parts of the country, until the end of the fifteenth century.

These seven centuries, although never without sporadic fighting for territory and domination, were a most remarkable period of unity, a time when Christians, Jews, and Moslems lived in mutual tolerance and a measure of peace.

Spain was indeed the geographical and cultural crossroads of civilization.

Because one's culture—his value system and beliefs, his habits and customs, his skills, his arts—goes wherever he goes and is particularly intensified when he is part of a minority in a new environment, it is no surprise that Spain is, even today, a many-faceted land and that as the varied groups accommodated to each other and were assimilated over the centuries, elements of each were retained in a kind of mosaic pattern—many colors, many textures placed in juxtaposition to form a kaleidoscopic unity.

So also did the Spaniard of the sixteenth and seventeenth centuries bring to the New World his culture, gleaned from these many sources within his homeland, as he imposed his religion and way of life on the natives he found in this new land, and as he began to establish his own new life.

First, before mid-century in the 1500's, came the explorers, those committed to adventure and to the search for treasure and honor for their King. With them were the friars, Franciscans in the earliest years, who were at least equally committed to the search for pagan souls to save for their God.

The first Spanish families arrived in northern New Mexico and began to settle in, near the Indian pueblo of San Juan, in 1598. Their new life was rigorous. They suffered from isolation and loneliness, poverty, a constant battle with the vagaries of the weather, and difficulties with the people whose land it had been before the Spanish came. There were physical and cultural incursions by other groups, particularly the "Anglos," who centuries later were to bring no less zeal with their hopes to convert than had the Franciscan missionaries, even though that to which they wished to convert the Spanish was not necessarily, or often, God. Small wonder that the early comers—and their descendants—tried to preserve their own cultural memories, values, and expressions.

Today we see in New Mexico the adobe flat-roofed houses and the *hornos* which the Moslems gave to Spain; we hear proverbs which are common among Sephardic Jews and in the speech of *Don Quixote*; we see works of inlaid straw and *azulejo* tiles matching in design and color those found in Granada; we see performances of *Los Moros y los Cristianos*; we see religious art reminiscent of El Greco and Zurbarán; we see evidence of the deep, often dark, religious devotion found almost universally among Hispanics; of the *Hermanos* and the self-flagellation which their ancestors practiced and modern Spaniards still practice in the streets of Sevilla during *semana santa*; we pay reverence to the Virgin of Guadalupe who appeared to a young shepherd in Extremadura more than three centuries before she appeared to Juan Diego in Mexico and to whose patronage the American explorations were entrusted.

And we still find some of the *canciones* and *romances*, the *bailes* and *juegos,* the *cuentos* and *versos* and *leyendas* which were sung and danced and played centuries ago, some still remarkably intact, others changed with the years and the environment and the whims of human memory.

Much of this lore is for children. Hispanics, like members of every other ethnic society, have found in their arts a means of teaching as well as entertainment for their young, for these expressions of the people often retell their cultural history or articulate meanings far deeper than might be apparent at first blush. It is these pieces of children's folklore—some of the games, songs, stories, rhymes and legends which retain notable kinship with their counterparts in Spain and which are still known in New Mexico—that are addressed here. Some seem to have come directly to New Mexico from Spain. Others, perhaps even earlier imports to the western hemisphere, appear to have been first in Mexico, where Spaniards lived most of the sixteenth century before settlement began in New Mexico. A few others undoubtedly were first sung and danced here in their new world, beginning a new body of customs and folkways while still holding to the language and spirit of Spain.

The years of childhood are the long years, the shaping years, the time for implanting cultural memory. Robert Fulgham wrote a book whose title captured enough millions of readers to make it a bestseller, *All I Ever Needed to Know I Learned in Kindergarten*.

Carl Orff, twentieth-century composer and founder of *Schulwerk*, an elemental approach to music and movement education, said, referring to very early childhood:

> Everything that a child of this age experiences, everything in him that has been awakened and nurtured, is a determining factor for the whole of his life. Much can be destroyed at this age, much can remain undeveloped that can never be reclaimed.[3]

Perhaps those who came before, *los viejitos,* sensed this as a truth requiring their faithful preserving and handing down to the generations that followed this folklore which defined their culture and assured its continued life. Perhaps they knew that what is learned in childhood—the earlier the better—is that which stays longest and deepest in the mind, especially if it is learned through play.

The incursion of the entertainment media may be the final and fatal blow to much of the old lore, hence the continuing need for preservation of its parts, not, one hopes, as artifacts but as vibrant parts of the life of a culture.

VERSOS: RHYMES AND VERSES

El refrano español...condensa el saber del Viejo Mundo.[4]
The Spanish proverb...condenses the lore of the Old World.

To speak in metaphor and simile, to put significant, often profound truths into the fewest possible words are characteristics of Spanish conversation. Hundreds of *dichos*, or *refranes*, exist in everyday spoken Spanish as well as in Spanish literature. There are many collections readily available, and for that reason as well as the fact that they are less prominent in children's folk vocabulary than other forms, they are not included in this collection.

Closely related to these language-enhancing proverbs, however, are the *versos*, which, like them, make economical use of words and are expressions close to the heart and spirit of the people. They are filled with simple rhymes and assonance, are usually metered, and are often nonsensical. A number of those which follow are traceable to Old World counterparts.

SANA, SANA,
colita de rana,
si no sanas hoy,
sanarás mañana.[5]

Heal, heal,
little tail of the frog,
if you don't heal today,
you'll heal tomorrow.

ADIÓS, ADIÓS
que te vaya bien,
que le trampe el tren,
que te machuque bien.[6]

Goodbye, goodbye,
have a good trip,
get hit by a train,
get well smashed up.

SAN ANTONIO BENDITO,
tres cosas te pido:
salud, dinero,
y un buen marido.

Blessed St. Anthony,
three things I ask of you:
health, money,
and a good husband.

PATITO, PATITO,
color de café
si usted no me quieres,
yo no sé por que.
Me gusta la leche,
Me gusta el café,
pero más me gustan
los ojos de usted.[7]

Little duck,
color of coffee,
if you don't love me,
I don't know why.
I like milk,
I like coffee,
but I like better
your eyes.

HEA, HEA, HEA,
ya parió la Andrea
cuatro cochinitos
y un costal de brea.[8]

Hea, hea, hea,
Andrea has given birth
to four little pigs
and a bag of tar.

CHATO NARATO
narices de gato:
subites al cerro,
narices de perro:
bajates al plan,
narices de gavilán[9]

Snub-nosed one,
nostrils of a cat:
climb the hill,
nostrils of a dog:
go down to the plain,
nostrils of a hawk.

NIÑO, NIÑO, NIÑO,
patos de cochino,
nano, nano, nano,
patos de marrano.[10]

Child, child, child,
feet of a pig,
nano, nano, nano,
feet of a pig.

BATE BATE CHOCOLATE
con arroz y con tomate.
uno, dos, tres, CHO,
uno, dos, tres, CO,
uno, dos, tres, LA,
uno, dos, tres, TE,
chocolate, chocolate,
chocolate, chocolate.

Beat beat the chocolate
with rice and tomato.
one, two, three, CHO,
one, two, three, CO,
one, two, three, LA,
one, two, three TE,
chocolate, chocolate,
chocolate, chocolate.

EL APACHE Y EL COMANCHE
se fueron pa' Santa Fe
a vender a sus hijitas
por azúcar y café.[11]

The Apache and the Comanche
left for Santa Fe
to sell their little daughters
for sugar and coffee.

PIN MARÍN DE DON PINGUÉ
Cácara mácara pípiri fué.
A-E-I-O-U
¡El burro sabe más que tu![12]

Pin marín de don Pingué
Cácara mácara pípiri fué.
A-E-I-O-U
The burro knows more than you!

LOS POLLITOS DICEN
pió, pió, pió,
cuando tienen hambre,
cuando tienen frio.
La mamá les busca
el maiz y el trigo,
Les da su comida
y les presta abrigo.[13]

The little chickens say
pió, pió, pió,
when they are hungry,
when they are cold.
The mother looks for
the corn and the wheat,
she gives them food,
and she gives them shelter.

CANCIONES: SONGS

Él que canta sus males espanta. [14]
He who sings frightens his troubles away.

   Singing has always been such an integral part of Spanish cultural tradition that it is not surprising to find in the Southwest an abundance of songs which have constantly increased since the arrival of the Spanish colonists at the end of the sixteenth century. These early settlers brought with them the songs that were current in their day. They continued to sing the old songs and also composed new ones, thus keeping alive the old repertoire and enlarging it in succeeding generations. [15]

O nly three representative *canciones infantiles* are presented here: a *romance,* a *canción,* and a series of *cunas.* The *romance,* probably the oldest Spanish folksong form found in the Americas, is a ballad, a narrative. It is a direct ancestor of the *corrido,* a particularly Mexican form which often tells a story based on a specific event in time. The *canción* is usually a gentler and more personal song. The *cuna* is simply a lullaby.
   Excellent collections of these types of songs, as well as the many other forms of Spanish folksong—at least as they exist in modern form— can easily be found.

EL SEÑOR DON GATO

   The *romance* here, directly traceable to Spain, seems to have undergone few changes in its story line, to "have lost little in the handling," according to Aurora Lucero-White Lea. She writes further, "No doubt this is due to the fact that, comparatively speaking, this type of ballad is short, the language simple, and the story contained therein, if it can be called a story, inconsequential." [16]
   Inconsequential or not, *El Señor Don Gato,* has found favor with countless children in the Southwest since Spanish colonial times, and today it is a popular addition to music textbooks throughout the country, along with its "singable translation." As one comes to expect, the tunes differ widely; I have at least a dozen distinct tunes for the story of this amorous cat, and there are doubtless many more. Word variants exist, but the story remains the same in all but one of its most important elements.

Don Gato is a cat in love. In his eagerness to reach his beloved, he falls from the roof and suffers fatal injuries. In the Spanish version he calls for a doctor; in the most complete New Mexican version he calls for a priest. Don Gato is mourned by some, but the mice celebrate his passing by dressing themselves in red.

The Spanish story gives more details about his injuries: broken head, broken spine, broken ribs—seven in some accounts, three in others. It also has a distinctly different ending: as he is being carried through the streets—sometimes *la calle del pescado* (the street of the fish)—for burial, the overwhelming odor of sardines brings Don Gato back to life:

Por eso dice la gente:	Therefore the people said:
_Siete vidas tiene un gato.[17]	"A cat has seven lives."

In the New Mexico version such a resurrection does not occur. Here are the words for a version of the Spanish *romance* known in many areas of northern New Mexico:

Estaba el gatito prieto	There was a dark cat
en una silla sentado	seated in a chair
con su media de pelillo	with his fuzzy stockings
y un zapato alpargatado.	and his fiber shoe.
Le han llegado las noticias	They had brought the news
que había de ser casado	that he would be marrying
con una gata morita,	a spotted cat,
hija del gato bragado.	daughter of a tough cat.
El gato de pura alegría	The cat from pure happiness
se cayó de arriba abajo.	fell down from the top.
Se ha quebrado la cabeza	He had broken his head
y la mitad del espinozo.	and the middle of his spine.
Traíganle quién le confiese	They brought a confessor
al gatito enamorado.	to this little enamored cat.
_Confieso a mi confesor	"I confess to my confessor
que he sido un gato malvado	that I have been a wicked cat
y si d' esta no me escapo	and if I can't escape this,
que no me entierren en sagrado;	don't bury me in sacred ground;
entiérrene me en un arroyo,	bury me in an arroyo.
donde me pise el ganado,	where the livestock will walk on me,
que digan los gachupines,	let the fellows say,
_Aquí murió el malhadado;	'Here died the unlucky one;
no murió de tabardillo,	he didn't die of sunstroke,

ni de dolor de costado,
murió de un dolor de amor
que le dió desperado.
Los ratones que lo saben
se visten de colorado.[18]

nor of a pain in the side;
he died of the pain of love
that he gave desperately.'"
The mice that found out about it
were seen dressed in red.

A number of representative tunes follow; all of them can be adapted to the words given here—if a refrain is added. Since a refrain is a part of all the Spanish versions, it is likely that some sort of refrain was also a part of the New Mexican version in earlier times.

DON GATO
Example 1

Castilblanco, Spain

DON GATO
Example 2

Laina, Spain

DON GATO
Example 3,

Companario, Spain

Sen - ta - do en si - lla de o - ro; _____ es -
ta - ba el se - ñor don Ga - to _____ con u - na me -
dia de se - da _____ y u - no za - pa - ti - llo
blan - co. A - le y a - le - pún, a - le y a - le - pún, u -
no za - pa - ti - llo blan - co. _____

DON GATO
Example 4

San Pedro Manrique, Spain

Es - ta - ba el se - ñor don Ga - to, es - ta - ba el se -
ñor don Ga - to sen - ta - di - to en su te - ja - do, que ru - miau miau,
miau, que ru - miau miau miau.

DON GATO
Example 5

New Mexico

Es - tan-do el se- ñor don Ga - to, es - tan-do el se- ñor don Ga - to sen-ta - di-to en un te - ja - do, sen-ta - di-to en un te - ja - do. Ha re-ci-bi-do u - na car - ta que su quie-re ser ca - sa - do con u-na ga-ta mon - te - sa so - bri - na de un ga - to par-do. A - le y a - la-pun, a - le y a - la-pun, ¡So - bri-na de un ga - to par - do! A- le y a - la- pun, a - le y a - la- pun ¡So - bri-na de un ga - to par - do!

Example 5 is the only setting attributed to a New Mexico origin by the renowned collector of Hispanic folk music in the Southwest, John Donald Robb.[19] Its kinship to many of the Spanish tunes is obvious.

A LA PUERTA DEL CIELO

This *canción* could easily be classified a *cuna*. It does, however, seem to be an introspective, personal statement by the mother, at least in some of its manifestations. It, too, has covered the distance between Europe and America across the years, and a number of interesting examples of its metamorphosis are shown here.

The oldest versions are probably these two from Spain, the first a well known children's song in Extremadura:

Pajarito que cantas en la laguna, no despiertes al niño que está en la cuna. Ea la nana, ea la nana, duérmete lucerito de la mañana.	Little bird singing at the lake, don't wake the child in the cradle. Ea la nana, ea la nana, sleep little light of the morning.

A los niños que duermen Dios los bendice,	God bless the children who are sleeping,
A las madres que velan Dios las asiste.	God bless the mothers who are watching.
Ea la nana, ea la nana,	Ea la nana, ea la nana,
duérmete lucerito de la mañana[20]	sleep little light of the morning.

PAJARITO QUE CANTAS EN LA LAGUNA
Example 1

Spain

The next version, with words identical to the second verse of the first example, is melodically quite different in mode and mood. It comes from Medinaceli in Spain.

A LOS NIÑOS QUE DUERMEN
Example 2

Spain

Next, from South America, is *Canción de Arrulla*:

En la puerta del cielo   At the gate of heaven
venden zapatos   they are selling shoes
para los angelitos   for the little angels
que andan descalzos.[21]   who are going barefooted.

EN LA PUERTA DEL CIELO
Example 3

Finally comes the version which has been known and loved in northern New Mexico for many years.

A LA PUERTA DEL CIELO
Example 4

The Spanish lullaby shares certain elements with lullabies of every culture: a steady, rocking flow, a moderate tempo, a quiet and soothing delivery. The Spanish lullaby, however, has a character peculiarly its own: *el coco*.

We have no description of this bogey-man. No one seems ever to have actually seen him. But he is a very real being in many lullabies, albeit a figure of imagination, and the purpose he serves is clear: *If you don't go to sleep, el coco will come!* Another fearful creature found in Spanish lullabies is *la loba* (the wolf). Though they seem to be related, each appears to have its own special function; *el coco* checks for children who aren't asleep, and *la loba* is interested in those who are crying. The nature of the songs, especially the tunes, leads one to believe these were relatively gentle threats.

Gil writes in his monumental *Cancionero de Extremadura, "Uno de los rasgos más comunes para hacer dormir al niño consiste en infundirle miedo: 'mira que viene la loba' (probablemente símbolo astral de fecundidad) o 'que viene el coco' figura fantasmal imaginada."*[22] (One of the most common characteristics to make the child go to sleep is to instill fear: 'watch out for *la loba*' [probably an astral symbol of fertility] or 'let *el coco* come,' imaginary figure of fantasy.)

Gil gives a number of examples from the oral tradition in Extremadura which illustrate this. An interesting difference is seen in the first example in the words sung to *el niño* in the first verse and to *la niña* in the second.

DUERMETE NIÑO CHIQUITO

El Coco, Example 1

Fuenalabrada, Spain

Duér-me-te, ni-ño chi-qui-to,_____ mi-ra que vie-ne la lo-ba_____
Es mi ni-ña tan bo-ni-ta,_____ que pa-re-ce u-na ma-ce-ta,_____

pre-gun-tan-do_en ca-sa_en ca-sa,_____ ¿Quién es el ni-ño que llo-ra?_____
y su ma-dre me pa-re-ce_____ un ra-mo de vi-o-le-ta_____

Duér-me-te, mi ni-ño, que vie-ne el co-co,

se lle-va a los ni-ños que duer-men po-co.

Not surprisingly, *el coco* made his way to the Americas. In Chile we find the following:

Duérmete, niño mio,   Sleep, my child,
que viene el coco,   or el coco will come,
y se lleva a los niños   and he carries away the children
que duermen poco.[23]   who sleep only a little.

By the time he reached Santa Fe he had grown more menacing, as this example indicates:

Alarru, mi hijito,   Lullaby, my little child,
duérmase ya;   go to sleep now;
que viene el coco   or el coco will come
y se lo comerá.[24]   and eat you up.

An example from Las Placitas not only warns about el coco but also invokes Santa Ana and San Joaquin to help in lulling the child to sleep:

Señora Santa Ana,   Santa Ana,
Señor San Joaquin,   San Joaquin,
arrulla este niño   lull this child
que quiere dormir.   who wants to sleep.
Duérmete, niñito,   Sleep, little child,
duérmete nomás   sleep or else
que hay viene el coco   el coco will come
y te comerá.[25]   and eat you up.

Unfortunately, the records which give the words for the New Mexico versions rarely give the musical notation. The following musical example, *Canción de Cuna,* comes from San Martín de Trevejo in Spain, but it is appropriate for the words above.

SEÑORA SANTA ANA
El Coco, Example 2

San Martin de Trevejo, Spain

Se - ño-ra San - ta A-na, Se-ñor San Joa quin, a-rru-lla es-te

ni-ño que quie - re dor- mir. Duér-me-te, ni-ñi-to, duér-me-te no-más

que hay viene el co - co y te co-me - rá.

Here are a few more examples of particularly lovely melodies from Spain which are *cuna* settings for calling *el coco*.

DUERMETE NIÑO MIO
El Coco, Example 3

Murcia, Spain

Duér-me-te ni - ño mio,_____ que viene al co - co_____ y se lleva a los

ni-ños_____ que duer-men po - co._____ po - co._____

DUERMETE NIÑO CHIQUITO
El Coco, Example 4

Fuenalabrada, Spain

Duér - me-te ni - ño chi - quito,_____ que vie-ne el lo - bo y la

lo-ba_____ pre - gun-tan-do en ca-sa en ca-sa_____

a ver los ni - ños que duer-men._____

DUERMETE MI NIÑO
El Coco, Example 5

Extremadura, Spain

Duér-me - te, mi ni-ño, que vie-ne la lo - ba, y vie-ne di - cien-do:

¿Quién es el que llo - ra? ¡Ha-la! ro, ro, ro, que ya se dur - mio.

DUERME, NIÑO, DUERME
El Coco, Example 6

Extremadura, Spain

Duer-me, ni - ño, duer - me, duer-me, que vie-ne el co - co

y se lle-van los ni - ños que duer-men po - co.

-21-

JUEGOS: GAMES

El destino de las culturas se lee en sus juegos. [26]
The destiny of the cultures is read in their games.

It should be noted that children at play are not playing about; their games should be seen as their most serious-minded activity. [27]

Play is a child's answer to life. Through play he learns the limits and possibilities of his two worlds, the world inside himself and the outer world in which he lives.

From the beginning of life until its end the instinct for play is present—and strong. It is reflected in the infant's responsive smile when he is tickled under the chin, in the toddler's gleeful clapping when he knocks down a column of blocks he has just built up, in the older child's careful adherence to the exact formula of an ancient game. No less is it reflected in the octogenarian's pleasure in working a difficult puzzle or participating in a rowdy board game. And of course there exists the wide world of active games and sports in which millions of all ages participate actively and/or passively, but we are not dealing with these games here.

There are many values intrinsic to the games of childhood. Games help to "civilize" children. They give them opportunities to express their energies and emotions in acceptable ways; to cope with unexpected circumstances and to adapt; to imitate the activities of adulthood—cooking, hammering, playing mother, playing fireman; to enter the world of fantasy and to stretch the imagination to vast limits; to explore and experiment. Games are dynamic ways of teaching cultural values, even spiritual development. They reflect the archaic stages of the development of mankind with their ancient language, their magic formulas, their rules and customs which arose from long-forgotten sources. The elemental building stones that are dominant in games, that create their enchantment for children, include such things as risk, fate, make believe, and sometimes a delicious sense of panic that almost erases reality temporarily.

Here are games, including variants of some of them, which have been played in many areas where there are communities of Spanish-speaking people. The origins of most of them can be traced to Spain. Others appear to be indigenous to New Mexico and southern Colorado. There are games one plays with an infant, finger-counting games, hand games, singing games, games which entail dramatic action. Some have come down to us remarkably intact. Others show slight changes from earlier versions. Many of them vary in minor detail from country to country within the Americas as well as, often, from community to community in New Mexico, but the essence of the culture remains. A Spanish cultural anthropologist writes, "The different cultures will be reflected in the games they practice, these games will show the essential and well-defined characteristics of those cultures."[28]

GAMES WITH RHYMES, CHANTS

Movement is intrinsic to the earliest games of children, and it is in fact their earliest medium for learning. Phyllis Weikart, movement research specialist, believes a child's motor skill development is greatly enhanced by creating opportunities for emphasizing steady beat long before he is old enough to be consciously aware of it.[29] The ability to maintain a steady beat lies at the root of all other motor skill development, a crucial part of the child's total development, and such beat-keeping never fails to delight young children. The emphasis in the following games is the beat.

LANZA, LANZA

In this game played with the very young, guaranteed to bring forth laughter, the player makes a circle in the air over the child's mid-section and at the appropriate words pokes him in the stomach. This may be native to New Mexico.

Lanza, lanza,	Spear, spear,
pícale la panza.[30]	to bite (poke) you in the stomach.

Here is an obvious variant, also from Santa Fe:

Lanza, lanza,	Spear, spear,
si no te ries,	if you don't laugh,
te pico la pansa.[31]	I'll poke you in the stomach.

LOS DOS PATITOS

Here is a game played with the baby's feet, moving first one then the other to the beat of the verse:

Estas dos patitas	These two little feet
jueron (fueron) a cortar lemitas	went to cut squawberries;
corre la una, corre la otra,	one runs, the other runs.,
corren las dos juntitas.[32]	the two run together.

Differing from the above only in what is to be gotten and the method of getting it is a second rhyme for playing with the baby:

Estos piecitos	These little feet
fueron a robar meloncitos;	went to steal melons;
en la huerta de su papacito.	in the garden of their daddy.
Corre el uno, corre el otro,	one runs, the other runs,
corren los dos juntitos.[33]	the two run together.

CABALLITO

This foot-dandling game is played by seating the child astride the player's foot; player and child face each other. (For the slightly older child and a more boisterous finish the child sits with his back to the player, both facing the same direction.) The player holds the child's hands firmly and bounces him up and down to the beat of the verse. On the final line, with the player still holding his hands, the child is "bucked" off the "horse."

Caballito, caballito,	Little horse, little horse,
no me tumba, no me tumba,	don't tumble me off, don't tumble me off,
a galope y a galope,	galloping and galloping,
recio, recio, recio.	hurry, hurry, hurry.
¡Que viva San Antonio![34]	Long live St. Anthony!

EL BORRIQUITO

The words for this game from Spain are similar to a North American Spanish singing game, El Burrito, which is discussed later. This spoken game is similar to Caballito: a young child is placed astride one's knee or ankle, and bounced in beat to the chanted rhyme:

Arre borriquito,	Hurry, little donkey,
vamos a Belén,	we are going to Bethlehem,
que manaña es Pascua	tomorrow is Easter
y el otro también.[35]	and the other also.

Another version, also from Spain, calls for a first verse to be played as above and a second, during which one moves his hands back and forth before the child's face.

(1) Arre, caballito, que vamos a Belén, arre, arre, arre, que yegamah (llegamos)tarde.	Hurry, little horse, we are going to Bethlehem, hurry, hurry, hurry, we'll arrive late.
(2) Palmah, palmitah, higos y cositas; palma, palmones, higos y beyotones (bellotones).[36]	Palm, little palm, figs and little things; palm, big palms, figs and little acorns.

TORTITAS

Similar to "pat-a-cake" rhymes in other cultures are the following two verses, the first from Spain, the second its descendant in New Spain:

Tortitas y más tortitas, para madre las más bonitas, roscones y más roscones, para padre los coscorrones.[37]	Little cakes and more little cakes, for mother the prettiest, breads and more breads, for father blows on the head.

In Spain, although a *torta* is a cake, a *tortilla* is an omelet rather than the flat bread known by that name in Hispanic cultures of North America.

Tortillitas, tortillitas,
tortillitas para papá;
tortillitas, tortillitas,
tortillitas para mamá;
tortillitas de salvado
para papá cuando está
   enojado;
tortillitas de manteca
para mamá cuando está
   contenta.[38]
	Little tortillas, little tortillas,
	little tortillas for daddy;
	little tortillas, little tortillas,
	little tortillas for mama;
	little tortillas of bran
	for daddy when he is angry;
	
	little tortillas of butter
	for mama when she is happy.

APLAUDIMOS

This is a clapping game for very young children. They can respond to the rhyme with their whole bodies as well as simply with their hands.

Por arriba,	Reach up,
por abajo,	reach down,
por el lado,	to the side,
por el otro.[39]	to the other.

EL HUEVO

From Zafra, Spain, comes the first example of this game of naming the fingers or toes, similar to "This Little Pig Went to Market," but beginning at the opposite side of the hand or foot, touching first the little finger or toe.

Éste, compró un huevo.	This one bought an egg.
Éste, lo puso al fuego.	This one put it to the fire.
Éste, lo echó la sal.	This one put on salt.
Éste, lo probó.	This one tasted it.
Y este pícaro gordo se lo comió.[40]	And this fat rascal ate it up.

J. Manuel Espinosa reports finding both in Spain and in New Mexico the following variant:

Éste se jalló (halló) un huevito.	This one found a little egg.
Éste lo echó a frír (freir).	This one put it to fry.
Éste lo meneó.	This one scrambled it.
Éste lo echó sal.	This one put salt on it.
Y este viejo cuzco se lo comió.[41]	And this old stingy one ate it up.

Another way to play the game, using the same verso, is for any number of players to spread their fingers, with palms down on a table in front of them. The leader, or IT, points with a switch to each finger on the operative word of the phrase. When he comes to the final line, *se lo comió,* he tries to strike the outstretched thumb with his switch. The child who owns that thumb tries to pull it inside his hand before the switch can touch it. If the switch touches the thumb, the player is out. The game continues, repeating the *verso* until there is only one remaining player, who becomes the new leader.

The same counting game, but using a chicken instead of an egg, is found in California in these words:

Éste mató un pollito.	This one killed a little chicken.
Éste puso el agua a calentar.	This one put the water to heat.
Éste lo peló.	This one plucked it.
Éste lo guisó.	This one cooked it.
Y éste se lo comió.[42]	And this one ate it up.

Finally, from Texas, comes this straightforward version of a finger-naming game that mentions neither eggs nor chickens:

Niño chiquito,	Cute little child,
señor de anillos,	ringman,
tonto y loco,	foolish and crazy,
lambe caseulas,	licker of pots,
mata piojos.[43]	killer of lice.

LOS MADEROS DE SAN JUAN

Two players are seated facing each other. Holding hands, they rock back and forth according to the beat while saying the *verso*. At the end, each pulls backward from the other, stretching as far as possible until their hand clasp breaks. A tickling episode follows.

This was an enormously popular rhyme if one can judge popularity by widespread occurrence. In Zafra the words are:

Recotín, recotán,	Recotín, recotán,
los maderos de San Juan.	the timbers of St. John.
Unos piden vino	Some ask for wine
y otros piden pan.	and others ask for bread.
Recotín, recotín, recotán.[44]	Recotín, recotín, recotán.

Espinosa writes that the rhyme is identical in certain other parts of Extremadura except for the second line, which is changed to *las campanas de San Juan* (the bells of St. John). Reportedly popular also in Sevilla, the words are the same except for the first and last lines which become *Aserrín, aserrán* and *Aserrín, aserrín, aserrán*. There is evidence of the existence of this rhyme in the seventeenth century.

Among the many versions from New Mexico is this one collected by Espinosa:

¡Rique, rique, riquesón!	Rique, rique, riques_n!
Las inditas de San Juan	The little Indians of San Juan
piden pan y no les dan.	ask for bread and they
	don't give it to them.
Piden queso y les	They ask for cheese and they
dan un hueso,	give them a bone,
y se sientan a llorar	and they sit down to cry
en las trancas del corral	on the bars of the corral.
¡Tan, tan, tan! [45]	Tan, tan, tan!

Another from New Mexico finds "them" bemoaning their fate in a different place:

...y se ponen a llorar	...and they place themselves to cry
en la puerta del zaguán.	on the gate of the entrance hall.
Dan, dan, daran.	Dan, dan, daran.

An Arizona version addresses the issue of tickling:

Reque, reque, requesón,	Reque, reque, requesón,
pide pan y no le dan.	he asks for bread and they don't
	give it to him.
Pide queso y le	He asks for cheese and they
dan un hueso	give him a bone
pa' que se rasque	
el pescuezo. [46]	so he can scratch his neck.

Requesón is a rich, smooth cheese made from the whey left from a primary cheese.

PUN PUÑETE (also THE ANT IN THE BOX)

It is hard to find the origin of this game, for it is known by many names and is played in one form or another by children all over the world. A Spanish version from Zafra is the first one to be looked at:

One child is leader; the others stack their fists on top of each other, forming a column. The leader touches each fist, starting at the bottom, as he and the players carry on this dialogue:

¿Cómo se llama éste?	What is the name of this one?
Pun, Puñete.	Fist.
¿Y éste?	And this one?

Cascabelete.	Rattle (or rattlesnake).
¿Y éste?	And this one?
Pun Puñete.	Pun Puñete.

This continues until the leader reaches the top. Then, placing his finger in the hollow of the top fist, he asks and that player answers:

¿Qué hay aquí dentro?	What is there in here?
Oro y plata.	Gold and silver.
Al que se ría, la matraca.	Whoever laughs, the rattle.

All then remove their stacked fists, inflate their cheeks, and begin to punch the air escaping from their mouths. The first one to laugh becomes *la matraca*. This player then kneels and hides his eyes in front of the leader, who holds up a certain number of fingers over the kneeling player's head. The player must guess the correct number or give a forfeit.[47]

In two New Mexico versions, the rules and playing formation are the same, but the dialogues differ. Players sit around a table and stack their fists atop each other. In the first version, the player next to the top starts the questioning and the top player answers:

¿Qué tienes hay?	What do you have there?
Un puño puñete.	A fist.
Tíralo lejos y date en la frente.	Throw it far away and hit yourself on the forehead.

The player with the top fist follows directions—removes his fist and hits his forehead. The procedure continues with the next two top players until there are only two players left. Then the bottom player asks and the only remaining player answers:

¿Qué tienes hay?	What do you have there?
Una cajita.	A little box.
¿Y dentro la cajita?	And inside the little box?
Una vivorita.	A little snake.
¿Qué hace?	What does it do?
Mete el dedo y verás que rieso muerde.	Put your finger in and you'll see how hard it bites.

The bottom player, who has answered that *una vivorita* is inside the box, now places his fingers crosswise, tucks in his thumb, and presses his fingernail on the inserted finger of the questioner. Some versions answer *una hormiguita* (a little ant) instead of *una vivorita*. [48]

The second version, often called Ant in the Box, uses a different dialogue but plays the game the same way:

¿Que traes allí?	What are you bringing there?
Puño Puñete.	A fist.
Levanta tu mano y pégate en la frente.	Lift your hand and slap your forehead.

When the player has slapped his forehead, the game continues:

¿Qué traes allí?	What are you bringing there?
Una cajita.	A little box.
¿Y a dentro de la cajita?	And inside the little box?
Una hormiguita.	A little ant.
¿Pica?	Does it sting?
Si, ¿Quieres ver?[49]	Yes, do you want to see?

LA TUTURULECA

In this hand game the players sit in a circle, hands outspread in front of them, palms down. The leader taps each of the players' fingers in succession, one finger per accented syllable. At *dedo* or *gallo* (to be decided before the game begins) the tapped finger is bent inside the hand, thus removing it from the game. When only one finger remains, the leader pinches it and makes it "fly away."

La tuturuleca	The half-blind one
pasó por aquí	passed by here
convivando	inviting
a todos sus amos,	all her masters,
menos a mí;	except for me;
cuchara, salero,	spoon, salt shaker,
esconde tu dedo,	hide your finger,
que te pica el gallo.	the rooster will peck it.
¡Se lo llevó el gavilán! [50]	The hawk will take it!

A variant of this verse, with no game rules attached, is as follows:

La tuerta culeca	The one-eyed brooding hen
pasó por aquí	passed by here
convivando	inviting
a todos sus amos	all her masters
menos a mí.[51]	except for me.

GAMES WITH DRAMATIC PLAY

In a way, all games can be thought of as little dramas. We poke the baby's stomach with a "spear," we let him ride the "little horse," we keep a "rattlesnake" in the "box." A degree of make-believe exists in almost all games. The next group, however, is different in that each has a real scenario as part and parcel of the game. There are specific characters, planned "homes," and formalized dialogue in most cases. An interesting note to these games is that the leader, *IT*, is now often referred to as the *mother*.

LOS COLORES (also TAN TAN and LA VIEJA INES)

This is another very old and very widely known game. A Spanish author writes, *"...[U]n mundo de antiguas leyendas, de literatura medieval...este juego de Zafra nos pone en contacto con la vieja dilíctica de buenos y malos, de cielo e infierno, de ángeles y demonios. Realmente es como si el tiempo se hubiera detenido en este juego."* [52] (...A world of ancient legends, of medieval literature...this game from Zafra places us in contact with the old dialogue of good and evil, of heaven and hell, of angels and demons. In reality it is as if time had stopped in this game.")

In the Spanish game, two groups stand some distance apart: hell, led by the devil, and heaven, led by an angel. Each leader gives each member of his group the name of a color. The devil approaches the kingdom of heaven and has the following conversation with the angel:

¡Pam, pam! ¿Quién es?	Knock, knock! Who is it?
El demonio pinchando papas con el tenedor.	The devil piercing potatoes with a fork.
¿Qué quieres?	What do you want?
Un color.	A color.
¿Qué color?	What color?
El color_____	The color_____

If one of the angel's team is named with the color given by the devil, that player must accompany the devil to his camp. If not, the devil returns alone, having lost this round. The above procedure is then reversed, with the angel trying to rescue a prisoner from hell. The conversation is the same except the angel, when asked who is there, answers *angel de la guarda* (angel of the guard). The winning side, when the game ends, is the side with the most players. [53]

A New Mexico version has a number of differences. Instead of two full teams, there are only an angel and a mother (who is sometimes called a rainbow). All the other players stand behind the mother, each having been given the name of a color. A spot is chosen for the angel's base. The angel approaches the mother, asking for a color, and if one of the players is named with this color, a race ensues. If the color reaches the base before the angel, he is given the name of a different color and is able to rejoin the game. If the angel beats him to the base, or catches him en route, the color is out of the game. The words follow:

Tan, tan.¿Quién es?	Knock, knock. Who is it?
El angel bueno.	The good angel.
¿Qué quieres?	What do you want?
Quiero colores.	I want colors.
¿Qué color quieres?	What color do you want?
Quiero color_____[54]	I want the color_____

In Tan Tan the leaders are a mother and a *comprador de colores* (buyer of colors). The game is played as above but with the following conversation:

Tan, tan. ¿Quién es?	Knock, knock. Who is it?
La vieja Inés (give a different answer each time).	Old lady Ines.
¿Qué quieres?	What do you want?
Un listón de _____[55]	A ribbon of _____,

La Vieja Inés is almost the same game. There is the mother and *La Vieja Inés*. The other players are the Mother's family, *los colores*. The children are lined up behind the Mother. *La Vieja Inés* approaches and knocks at the door:

Tan, tan.	Knock, knock.
¿Quién es?	Who is it?
La Vieja Inés.	Old Lady Ines.
¿Qué quieres?	What do you want?
Quiero colores.	I want colors.
¿Que color quieres?	What color do you want?
Quiero _____	I want _____

The selected color races *La Vieja Inés* to the base. If he reaches it first, he is given a new color name and is permitted to return to the game. If Inés catches him, he becomes her prisoner. When all the colors are prisoners, Inés must catch the mother.[56]

El COYOTITO Y LA ZORRA

The coyote and the fox are leaders, the coyote standing alone, the fox leading a chain of players who hold each other by their waists. The fox and her chain of *borreguitos* make a circle around the coyote, and the two principals engage in a dialogue as the coyote tries to get a little lamb away from the others:

San Miguel, dame un borreguito.	St. Michael, give me a little lamb.
¿Dónde está él que te di?	Where is the one I gave you?
Aquí lo tengo bajo al muela.	I ate it. (I have it here below my molar.)
Pues mira para el cielo (mientras da vuelta la zorra).	Well, look up at the sky (while the fox turns around).

At this point all the players shout to the coyote:

Tome patitas para que hagas posole.	If you're so hungry, try to catch some little feet for your soup. (Take little feet to make posole.)

Then the chase is on as the fox and her chain run as fast as they can, weaving this way and that to avoid the coyote who is trying to capture the last player in the chain.

In a variant of the game the principals are the coyote and the mother. As above, the players form a chain behind the mother. The coyote approaches the others who quickly join the head and tail of the line together, making a circle with the mother in the center. The mother hits at the coyote as he tries to pull a child from the circle. When one is pulled away, the mother and all the others give chase as the coyote tries to get the captured child to his home base.[57]

SEÑOR MARTINEJO

All players but one are seated in a circle, legs crossed, heads in hands, eyes hidden. The leader, *Señor Martinejo*, walks behind the players, outside the circle, swinging a handkerchief and chanting:

Zun zun de la calavera,	Zum zum on the drum (skull),
el guese duerme le doy una perla.	whoever sleeps I'll give him a pearl.

He drops the handkerchief behind someone and continues around the circle. If it is still there when he comes around again, he hits the player behind whom it had been dropped, picks up the handkerchief, and runs. The "awakened" player runs after *Señor Martinejo*, chasing him back to the empty place. Then between player and *el Señor* :

¿Dónde está el pan que te di?	Where is the bread I gave you?
Me lo comí.	I ate it.
¿Y si más te diera?	And if I gave you more?
Más comiera,	I would eat more.
¿Y el huevito?	And the little egg?
En el hoyito	In the hole.
¿Y la sal?	And the salt?

Here el Señor sits down in the empty place and answers:

En su santisimo lugar.	In your holy place.

The game begins again with the new *Señor Martinejo.* [58]

LA GALLINITA CIEGA

One player scratches in the dirt, looking for food. The other players circle around , questioning her:

Gallinita ciega, ¿qué anda haciendo?	Blind hen, what are you doing?
Ando buscando unos cunquitos.	I am looking for cornmeal crumbs.
¿Pa' quién?	For whom?
Pa' mis pollitos.	For my chicks.
¿Y me dará uno?	And will you give me one?
No.	No.
Pues piérdete.	Then get lost.

The blind hen chases the other players; the one caught is the next *gallinita.* [59]

An old game from Spain has the same title, but the procedure for playing and the dialogue are completely different from this New Mexico version. A requirement of the Spanish game is that the *gallinita* be blindfolded, and one suspects that this is also a part of the New Mexican game, even though the old sources do not mention a blindfold.

A variant in the verse, also found in New Mexico and Colorado, follows:

¿Qué andas buscando, gallina ciega?	What are you looking for, blind hen?
Cunques pa' mis pollitos.	Corn crumbs for my chicks.
¿Quése los pollitos?	Where are your chicks?
Están debajo 'e la artesa.⁶⁰	They are under the wooden bowl.

LA BRUJA

The next game is a well-structured drama based on a fairy tale from Spain. At least nine children must be involved: a witch, a mother and her seven children named for the days of the week. There are two bases: a cave for the witch and a home for the mother and her children.

In spite of a strict framework within which the play takes place, there is much opportunity for improvisational dialogue, unlike the previous games.

The mother tells her children they have nothing to eat and that she must go to the store for, for instance, potatoes. She tells *Domingo* to look after *Lunes* while she is gone. As soon as she leaves, *Domingo* goes to sleep, and the witch steals *Lunes*. When the mother returns, she is sad at the loss of the child and very angry at *Domingo's* irresponsibility. What could she have been doing? *Domingo* tells her mother the truth, and she is punished. She is a lazy bones (*flajón*), a sleepy head (*dormilón*).

The mother must return to the store, this time for some other food, perhaps coffee. She tells *Domingo* to look after *Martes* and especially not to fall asleep. This time *Domingo* stays awake, but her attention is on her game of marbles or some other specific game, and the witch steals *Martes*. The mother appears, discovers the truth, and reacts as before in sadness and anger.

This process continues. The mother continues to return to the store, each time for a different food, each time leaving *Domingo* in charge of the next child (*Miércoles, Jueves, Viernes, Sábado* in turn). Each time *Domingo* finds another activity so that she is distracted when the witch comes to steal the child. When only *Domingo* is left, the mother tells her to take care of herself. Of course, she is also stolen by the witch.

When the mother returns and finds all her children gone, she is distraught. She goes to the witch's cave, asking her if she has seen her children. All the seven children have now come out of the witch's cave, have their heads covered, and are representing different fruits. The witch, carrying a basket, answers yes, she had seen them running by the creek, but that had been some time ago. Would the mother like to buy the very nice fruit she carries in her basket?

The mother tries them, but each fruit has something wrong with it; for instance, the apple might be too sour, the pear too soft, the peach bitter, the melon green, the cherry spoiled, etc. After the mother has tried and rejected all of them, the witch sprinkles sugar on them and offers another taste. The mother then buys them all.

She then asks each fruit, "How did you get here?" The apple might answer, "On my feet." The mother responds, "Then go home on your feet." The "apple" then must walk back to the home. Each fruit is asked the same question; each gives a different answer; and each must go home according to that answer.

When all the "fruits" have been sent away, the mother returns and finds all her children safe at home.[61]

SINGING GAMES

Tonal notation is far less common than word notation, even in games classified as singing games. In addition, tonal memory is far less reliable than verbal memory. For these reasons, we find gaps in our assured knowledge of tunes that go with certain of the singing games. Some of the ten songs included here are often included in Mexican and other Latin American collections of children's games, but there are New Mexican Spanish variations which make their inclusion here appropriate. In a few cases, certain guesses have been made in relation to tunes which seem to belong with certain sets of words. Like the others, the singing games are often based on origins in Spain.

MATARILE (also AMBO HATO and AMÓ ATÓ)

"Este juego está documentado en obras literarias desde tiempo inmemorial" (This game is documented in literary works from time immemorial).[62] Possibly the most widely known children's game in the Spanish-speaking world, this has many variants in name and in details. Its origin is obscure.

In Medellín, Spain, all the players but one are *Princesas*; the other is *La Reina*. First the queen, then the princesses, approach each other and sing alternate verses, the queen singing odd-numbered verses, the princesses even. All players clap in time with the music. The princess named to find the keys in the sea becomes the next queen.

(1) Yo tengo un castillo,   I have a castle,
                 Matarile-rile-rile;
yo tengo un castillo,   I have a castle,
                 Matarile-rile-rile-ron, chimpón.

(2) Yo tengo otro,   I have another,
         Matarile-rile-rile;
yo tengo otro,   I have another,
       Matarile-rile-rile-ron, chimpón.

(3) El mío es major....   Mine is bigger....

(4) Que le vemos a hacer....   Let's see if it is....

(5) Romperemos una piedra....   We will break a stone....

(6) ¿Qué piedra va a ser?....   What stone is it going
                                  to be?....

(7) Romperemos a _____....   We will break _____....

(8) ¿Qué oficio le vamos a dar?   What occupation are we going
                                  to have?....

(9) Le daremos peluquera....   We will be hairdressers....
    (o otro oficio)   (or other occupation)

(10) Ese oficio si/no me gusta....   This occupation does/does not
                                  please me....
   (repeat this verse until the queen finds an occupation the
   princesses like.)

(11) ¿Con quién la casaremos?...   To whom shall we marry her?

(12) La casaremos con _____...   We'll marry her to _____....

(13) Ese chico no me gusta....   That boy doesn't please me....
    (Repeat until they agree on a person named.)

(14) Le daremos un castillo....   We will give you a castle....

(15) ¿Dónde están las llaves?....   Where are the keys?....

(16) En el fondo del mar....   In the bottom of the sea....

(17) ¿Quién baja a por ellos?....   Who will go down for them?

(18) Bajará _____......[63]   _____ will go down....

The most frequently heard tune, a tune to which these words can be adapted, is the following:

TENGO UN CASTILLO
Matarile, Example 1

Ten - go un cas - ti - llo, ma - ta - ri - le - ri - le.

Ten - go un cas - ti - llo, ma - ta - ri - le - ri - le - ron.

Next comes a version from New Mexico. Although there are many differences and a less complex story, the similarities to the Spanish game are evident. The above tune can also be used easily with these words. This version seems strangely incomplete. In order to balance the story line, a fifth verse not found in the original source has been added.

In this game there are two leaders: the mother and the *mensajero de la Corte Real* (messenger of the royal court). The leaders are inside a circle made up of all the other players. The mother and the messenger sing the questions and answers, and the other players sing the first verse, the last two verses and the refrain. When a player is chosen as the "flower," she joins the leaders inside the circle.

(1) Ambo hato   Ambo hato
         Matarile rili,
Ambo hato   Ambo hato
         Matarile rili ron.

(2) ¿Qué quiere usted?   What do you want?
         Matarile rili,
¿Qué quiere usted?   What do you want?
         Matarile rili ron.

(3) Quiero un paje....   I want a page....

(4) ¿Quiere _____?....   Do you want _____?....

(5) Yo quiero_____....   I want _____....

(6) ¿Qué nombre le pon-   What name shall we give her?....
     dremos?....

(7) Le pondremos _____....   We will give her _____....
     (name of a flower)

(8) Aquí está mi hija	This is my daughter
Matarile rili,	
con dolor de corazón,	with pain in her heart,
Matarile rili ron.	
(9) Celebremos,	Let's celebrate,
Matarile rili,	
Celebremos,	Let's celebrate,
Matarile rili ron.	
(10) Todos juntos en la unión,	All together,
Matarile rili,	
todos juntos en la unión,	all together,
Matarile rili ron.[64]	

Finally, here is a version from Mexico, with possible connection to France. In this game players are divided into two lines facing each other. Each line will advance in turn toward the center during the first phrase of the verse, then return to its place on the second phrase. The first verse should involve both lines advancing toward each other, then returning to their places.

(1) Amó ató,	Amó, ató.
Matarile-rile ró.	
Amó ató,	Amó, ató.
Matarile-rile ró.	
(2) ¿Qué quiere usted?	What do you want?
Matarile-rile ró.	
¿Qué quiere usted?	What do you want?
Matarile-rile ró.	
(3) Quiero un paje....	I want a page....
(4) Escoja usted....	Choose....
(5) ¿Qué oficio le pondremos?...	What job will you give her?
(6) Le pondremos lavandera....	We will make her a laundress....
(bordadora, etc.)	(embroiderer, etc.)
(7) Ese oficio no le gusta....	She doesn't like that job....
(8) La pondremos de sultana....	We will make her a sultan....
(9) Ese oficio sí le gusta....	She likes that job....

Here all the players join hands and sing as they go around in a circle:

Celebremos todas juntas,	Let's all celebrate together,
Matarile-rile-ró.	
Celebremos todas juntas,	Let's all celebrate together,
Matarile-rile-ró.[65]	

Here are two more tunes to which all the *matarile* songs can be adapted:

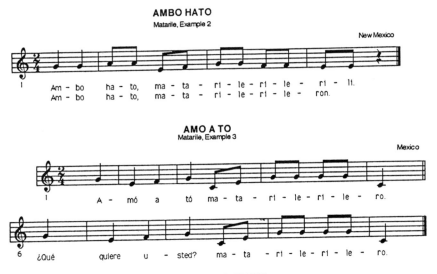

AMBO HATO
Matarile, Example 2

New Mexico

Am - bo ha - to, ma - ta - ri - le - ri - le - ri - 11.
Am - bo ha - to, ma - ta - ri - le - ri - le - ron.

AMO A TO
Matarile, Example 3

Mexico

A - mó a tó ma - ta - ri - le - ri - le - ro.

¿Qué quiere u - sted? ma - ta - ri - le - ri - le - ro.

EL REY Y LA REINA

This game is unmistakably a descendant of the *matarile* games detailed above, but its different name, its use of *pollitos* (chicks), and its different procedure seem to suggest that it should be considered separately.

There are a king and queen, and all the other players are *pollitos*. The king sings odd numbered verses and the queen even.

(1) Yo quiero una polla,	I want a chicken,
Matelili, lile, lila,	
Yo quiero una polla,	I want a chicken,
Matelili, lile, lilo.	

(2) Escójala usted,	Choose her,
Matelili, lile, lila,	
Escójala usted,	Choose her,
Matelili, lile, lilo.	

(3) Yo escojo a _____....   I choose _____....

(4) ¿Qué nombre le pondremos
    a la pollita?....

What name will you give the
chick?...

(5) Le pondremos _____....
    (Diamante fino, etc.)

We will give it _____....
(Fine diamond, etc.)

When one *pollito* is chosen, the king and queen form a ring around him and sing:

Celebremos,   Let's celebrate,
    Matelili lile lila,
Celebremos,   Let's celebrate,
    Matelili lile lilo.

The chosen player then joins the king and queen in the ring as successive *pollitos* are chosen with the same alternating king-and-queen questions and answers and celebrated with the verse above.

When all the *pollitos* have been chosen, the king and queen repeat the first two verses, then the king sings:

Yo escojo a la Reinita,   I choose the little queen,
    Matelili lile lila,
Yo escojo a la Reinita,   I choose the little queen,
    Matelili lile lilo.

Then all make a circle around the queen, singing:

Celebremos,   Let's celebrate,
    Matelili lile lila,
Celebremos,   Let's celebrate,
    Matelili lile lilo.[66]

This final tune, like the others, is quite suitable for singing the words or any of the *matarile* songs.

EL REY Y LA REINA (YO QUIERO UNA POLLA)
Matarile, Example 4

New Mexico

Yo quie - ro u - na po - lla, ma - te - li - le, li - le, li - la. Yo

quie - ro u - na po - lla, ma - te - li - le, li - le, li - lo.

JUAN PIRULERO (also JUAN MOLINERO and ANTÓN, ANTÓN PIRULERO)

He is called Antón in Spain, Juan in New Mexico; sometimes a piper, sometimes a miller, but the game is undoubtedly the same game. A circle of players is seated, singing, clapping the rhythm. A leader within the circle begins to imitate the playing of an instrument to one of the other players. That person must immediately mimic the action. If he is not paying attention, he must pay a forfeit. This continues as long as interest holds.

In Spain the words are:

Antón, Antón pirulero,	Anthony, Anthony piper,
cada cual, cada cual	each one, each one
atienda su juego,	pays attention to his game,
y el que no lo atienda	and he who doesn't pay attention to it
pagará una prenda.[67]	will pay a forfeit.

In New Mexico the game is usually played with the same seated circle. Each player chooses some activity—planting, shoemaking, sewing—and begins to mime it. Juan, whether he is *pirulero* (piper) or *molinero* (miller), usually pretends to play a flute or turn a millwheel. While all the players work at their tasks, Juan may at any point change his task to that of one of the other players. That player must immediately take up Juan's task. If the player is not paying attention and misses his cue, he must pay a forfeit and/or leave the game.[68]

I have seen children make interesting variations in the way they play this game; for instance, the inattentive player is consigned to turning the mill wheel (or playing the musical instrument) throughout the game, and Juan simply turns his attention to others. Another way is for the role of Juan to be passed each time he exchanges movements with a player.

JUAN PIRULERO

-42-

LA RUEDA DE SAN MIGUEL

This is a game which delights players of all ages—as long as they can keep going! Players stand in a circle, facing in, hands joined. A leader, also part of the circle, calls out the name of a player after *que se voltea* is sung. Then, with the circle still turning, the person called quickly turns to face outside the circle, continuing to hold hands with those on either side of him. The song and movement begin again, this time with one person facing outside the circle. The procedure continues until the leader has called each person, thus having all facing outside except the leader himself. Sometimes children end the game by having all the turned-out players sing the leader's name, and they go once around with all facing outside. The tempo increases each time the song is sung.

LA RUEDA DE SAN MIGUEL

Traditional

Rue-da, rue-da, San Mi-guel, San Mi-guel, to-do traen ca - mo-te y miel a lo ma-du-ro, a lo ma-du - ro, _____ de bu-rro.

In Spain the game is called *Turrutuntú* and has three sections. Section (A) is chanted while the players turn one by one, as above. When all are facing outside the circle, they chant section (B), during which the leader chooses two players who will stand back to back and bump each other as section (C) is chanted. Then the game begins again.

(A) Las cortinas de mi alcoba
    son de terciopelo azul;
    entre cortina y cortina
    se pasea un andaluz;
    coche de oro, _____
        para el moro,
    coche de plata, _____
        para la mata,
    Turruntuntú, _____ que
        vuelvas tú.

The curtains of my bedroom
are of blue velvet;
between the curtains
an Andalucian passes by;
coach of gold,_____
  for the Moor
coach of silver, _____ ,
  for the field,
Turruntuntú, _____,
  turn around.

(B) A los bollitos de miel,
    a los de San Miguel,
    a los de pan duro,
    que se vuelva _____ y _____

The little rolls of honey,
    those of San Miguel,
    those of hard bread,
    _____ and _____, turn around.

(C) Duro, duro, _____ con _____.[69]

Hard, hard, _____ with _____.

A slightly different version was given to me by a student who had come from Michoacan in central Mexico:

Hay vienen los burros de San
    Miguel, San Miguel
cargados de pura miel, de pura miel;
a la madura, a la madura,
_____ de burra, que se voltie.

The burros of St. Michael are
    coming
loaded with pure honey;
at maturity, at maturity,
_____ donkey, turn around.

The game is played the same way, but at the end, when all are facing outside the revolving circle, they begin a reversal process, calling the name of one who will turn back to face inside until all have made this move.[70]

EL BURRITO

Players stand in line and pretend to be riding burros as they sing. At the end of the song they bend over, and the last in line leaps over each of the others until he becomes head of the line. This continues until all have jumped over the others.

Arre, mi burrito,
que vamos a Belén,
que mañana es fiesta
y el otro tambien.
Arre, arre, arre,
lléveme usted al trote,
arre, arre, arre,
lléveme al galope.
De prisa, de prisa.[71]

Hurry, my little burro,
we are going to Bethlehem,
tomorrow is fiesta
and the other also.
Hurry, hurry, hurry,
carry me as we trot,
hurry, hurry, hurry,
carry me as we gallop.
Hurry up, hurry up.

The first tune below is for the verse above. The second is for El Borriquito found on page 24.

ARRE MI BURRITO
El Burrito, Example 1

New Mexico

A-rre mi bu - rri-to, que va-mos a Be- lén, que ma-ña-na es fle-sta y al

o- tro tam - bien. A-rre, a-rre, a-rre, lléve-me u - sted al tro-te;

a-rre, a-rre, a-rre, lléve-me al ga - lo-pe, de pri-sa, de pri-sa.

ARRE CABAYITO (EL BORRIQUITO)
El Burrito, Example 2

Spain

A - rre ca - ba - yi - to, que va - mos a Be - lén,
Que ma - ña - na eh fieh- ta, y al o - tro tam - bien.

A - rre, a - rre, a - rre, que ye - ga - moh tar - de.

LA VIUDITA DE SANTA ISABEL (also ARROZ CON LECHE)

As this game is played in New Mexico, one player is the little widow and another the priest's servant. These two stand facing each other in a circle made of all the other players. All players set the scene by singing the first two verses. The servant then sings the other verses while the players in the circle mimic the words and/or dance around the widow and the servant.

(1) Ésta es la viudita
de Santa Isabel
que quiere casarse
y no sabe con quién.

This is the little widow
of Santa Isabel
who wants to get married
and doesn't know to whom.

(2) El mozo del cura
le mandó un papel
y ella le mandó otro
de Santa Isabel.

The servant of the priest
sent her a paper
and she sent him another
from Santa Isabel.

(3) Corriendo, corriendo,	Running, running,
me di un tropezón,	I almost fell down,
por darle la mano	by giving my hand
le di el corazón.	I gave my heart.

(4) Me gusta la leche,	I like milk,
me gusta el café,	I like coffee,
pero más me gustan	but I like better
los ojos de usted.[72]	your eyes.

In another version sung in New Mexico, as well as in Mexico and Puerto Rico, the soloist is the only player inside the circle. There are a few differences in the words:

(1) Arroz con leche,	Rice with milk,
me quiero casar	I want to marry
con una viudita	a widow
de la capital.	from the capital.

(2) Que sepa coser,	Who knows how to sew,
que sepa bordar,	who knows how to embroider,
que ponga la aguja	who knows how to put the needle
en el campanal.	in the pincushion.

(3) Yo soy la viudita,	I am the widow,
la hija del rey,	the daughter of the king,
que me ando casando	I am getting married
y no encuentro con quién.	and I can't find out to whom.

(4) Contigo si,	To you yes,
contigo no,	to you no,
contigo mi vida,	to you, my life,
yo me he de casar.	I want to be married.

(5) Mi padre lo supo,	My father knows it,
de palos me dió,	he gave me a warning:
malaya sea el hombre	cursed be the man
que me abandonó.	who abandons me.

(6) Contigo si,	To you yes,
contigo no,	to you no,
contigo mi vido,	to you, my life,
yo me he de casar.[73]	I want to be married.

In Zafra an even number of children form a circle, and another child stands in the center as the little widow. Children in the circle sing as the widow touches a different child at each *ni contigo*. At *solo contigo* she embraces the child chosen, and all the others search for a partner. The odd one out is the next widow.

Soy viudita,	I am the little widow,
lo mando la ley;	controlled by the law;
quiero casarme	I want to get married,
no encuentro con quien.	I haven't met the person.
No es contigo, ni contigo,	It's not you, nor you,
ni contigo, ni contigo,	nor you, nor you,
solo contigo me casaré.[74]	only you will I marry.

The melody given here is simple, basic, and adaptable to all versions above. This game has had such popularity that its tune has stayed recognizable through its many arenas of activity. Although its meter is sometimes 4/4, sometimes 6/8, it retains sufficient similarity to be recognizable as the same song.

LA VIUDITA DE SANTA ISABEL

EL FLORÓN

A number of New Mexico versions of this game and its song exist. In the first version, all the players but one who is the guesser are seated in a line. The first player in line places a small ring, stone, or other token in one hand or the other, and the guesser must decide which hand holds it. If he is right, he trades places with the player. If he is wrong, the next child in line follows the procedure until the guesser finally is correct.

In another version, all but two players are seated, hands behind their backs. One of the other players is the guesser and one is the passer. The *florón* is taken by the passer to the hands of the seated players. He places it secretly in one child's hands. The guesser then must decide who

-47-

has it. If he is right, he takes that child's place in line, the passer becomes the guesser, and the child who had the stone *(el florón)* becomes the guesser. If the guess is wrong, the game continues with the same players. In New Mexico the song was sung with these words:

El florón está en las manos,	The flower is in the hands,
en las manos del Señor,	in the hands of the Lord,
el que no lo adivinaré	he who does not guess it
se queda pa' ton ton.[75]	is taken for a fool.

In Spain, from Castilblanco, the words are:

El florín ehtá (está) en la mano,	The flower is in the hand,
y en la mano ehtá el florín,	and in the hand is in the flower,
de la tuya va a la mía,	it goes from yours to mine,
de la mía ya pasó.	from mine I pass it on.
Florín, florín,	
florín, florón.[76]	

The following tune belongs to the Spanish version of the above words. The tune for the New Mexico version is not available, but if the two-line refrain is added to the New Mexico words, this setting becomes a very good and becoming fit. Its uneven phrase lengths make it a particularly charming tune.

EL FLORIN
El Florón, Example 1

Another version found in New Mexico is this one:

El florón anda en las manos,	The flower goes in the hands, in
en las manos,	the hands,
y en las manos le han de hablar,	and in the hands it has spoken,
adivine quién lo tiene, quién lo	guess who has it, who has it,
tiene,	
o se queda pa' ton ton.[77]	or be taken for a fool.

EL FLORON

El Florón, Example 2

New Mexico

El flo-rón an-da en las ma-nos, en las ma-nos, y en las ma-nos lo han de ha - llar, a - dí -ví - nen quién lo tie-ne, quién lo tie - ne, o se que - da pa' ton - tón.

This tune is found in Texas:

EL FLORON

El Florón, Example 3

Texas

El flo- rón es-tá en las ma-nos y en las ma-nos se ha de ha - llar. A-dí -ví - nen quien lo tie- ne o se que - da pa' plan - tón.

HILITOS DE ORO (also HEBRITOS DE ORO and ANGEL DE ORO)

Folklorist Arthur Campa says this ballad is very old and was widely diffused in the seventeenth century. The game is set up with the king's messenger (*mensajero*) and a mother with several daughters behind her. The messenger approaches, hopping on one foot and singing:

Hilitos, hilitos de oro
que se me vienen quebrando;
¿Qué dicen el rey y la reina
que tantas hijas tendrá?

Little threads of gold
that come to me broken;
What do the king and queen say
that you have so many
daughters?

The mother replies:

Que tenga las que tuviere
que nada le importa al rey

I may have many of them
but none is of importance to the
king.

-49-

The messenger leaves, hopping and singing:

Hilitos, hilitos de oro,	Little threads of gold,
yo ya me voy muy discontento,	I am leaving now very unhappy
a darle cuenta al rey.	to tell this story to the king.

The mother apparently rethinks her position, for she then sings:

Vuelva, vuelva, caballero,	Return, return, sir,
no sea tan discordal,	don't be so cross,
que de les hijas que yo tengo	of the daughters that I have
escoja la más mujer.	choose the one you want.

The messenger answers:

No escojo por bonita,	I don't choose for beauty,
ni tampoco por mujer,	neither for femininity,
yo escojo una florecita	I choose a little flower
acabada de nacer.	just born.

Then he goes to each daughter, pretending to smell her like a flower, and says,

Esa huele a rosa de castilla	This one smells like a rose of castille

and he goes down the line assigning each player a different flower. Finally he chooses the last one in line. The above procedure is repeated using birds, animals, or other objects instead of flowers. When he picks the last one, *la hija favorita,* he sings:

y a ti escojo, hija amada,	And I choose you, beloved daughter,
que le seas a la reina, criada.	to be the queen's maid.

The chosen player then stands against the wall, a piece of wood under her foot. Her mother asks her the following questions:

¿Tienes arroz?	Do you have rice?
No.	No.
¿Tienes frijoles?	Do you have beans?
No.	No.
¿Tienes pan?	Do you have bread?
No.	No.
¿Tienes carne?	Do you have meat?
¡Sí!	Yes!

The mother grabs the wood, and all players chase her.[78]

HILITOS DE ORO

New Mexico

Hi - li - tos, hi - li - tos de o-ro, que se me vie-nen que - bran-do; ¿qué di - cen el rey y la rei-na que tan - tas hi-jas ten - drá?

An incomplete version, played many years ago in New Mexico, is called *hebritos* rather than *hilitos,* both words with approximately the same meaning. In this version the dialogue is not in verse form, and the conversation has a few differences. The mother is called *Nana,* and there is the *hija querida* and the *mensajero.*

The messenger arrives, saying:

Naguelita, dice el rey que le dé una de sus hijas pa' que le alzo los cuartos. (Naguelita, the king says that you should give him one of your daughters for housekeeping.)
Nana replies:
Dile al rey que no las tengo pa' dar. (Tell the king that I don't have them to give.)
As he begins to leave, she asks him to return:

Vuelve, vuelve, caballero,	Return, return, sir,
no seas tan majadero.	don't be so stupid.

When he returns and begins to make his choices, he says the king wants kitchen help, gardening help, and people for other such chores. He finally chooses one who will be the queen's maid.[79]

VIBORA DE LA MAR

Here is a game which has stayed remarkably intact through its well-traveled life insofar as its words and rules are concerned. It seems to be played everywhere—Spain, Chile, Mexico, New Mexico. Its Anglo counterpart is *London Bridge Is Falling Down.* An interesting sidelight to this game is that it is not only for children, but is often used in events of celebration. A wedding or baptismal party, for instance, may begin with a long procession of attendants winding from church to home, singing *Víbora de la mar.*

Two children form an arch, each having chosen a fruit, for instance *melón* and *sandía*. All other players form a line, sometimes according to height, each holding the waist of the player ahead. They move under the arch until the end of the song, at which time the person passing through is captured. The victim then chooses, quietly, so as not to give the identities away, whether to go with the *melones* or the *sandias*, and gets behind the one he has chosen. When all have gone through this procedure, the two long lines have a tug of war.

In Mexico it is sung this way:

A la víbora, víbora	To the serpent, the serpent
de la mar, de la mar	of the sea, of the sea,
por aquí puede pasar.	it can pass here.
Los de adelante corren mucho,	Those in front run fast,
los de atrás se quedarán	those behind will stay
trás, trás, trás, trás.	behind, behind, behind, behind.
Una mexicana,	A Mexican girl,
de fruta vendita,	a fruit seller,
ciruela, chavacan,	plum, apricot,
melón o sandía.	cantaloupe or watermelon.
Será melón, será sandía,	It will be cantaloupe, it will be watermelon,
será la vieja del otro día,	it will be the old woman of
día, día, día,	another day,

Spoken:

¿Con quién te vas, con melón o con sandía?	With whom will you go, with watermelon or cantaloupe?

When all have cast their lot with one or the other, they pull apart as they chant:

El puente es de oro,	The bridge is made of gold,
el puente es de plata,	the bridge is made of silver,
el puente es de papel,	the bridge is made of paper,
el puente es de cáscara de plátano.[80]	the bridge is made of banana peeling.

VIBORA DE LA MAR
Example 1

Mexico

1 A la ví - bo - ra, ví - bo - ra de la mar, por a - quí pue - de pa- sar.

6 Los de a- de- lan- te co- rren mu- cho, los de a- trás se que- de- rán, tras, tras,

11 tras, tras U - na me - xí - ca - na de fru - ta ven - dí - ta, cí -

16 rue - la, cha - va - ca, me - lón o san dí - a. Se - rá me - lón, se -

21 rá san - día, se - rá la ví - e - ja del o - tro dí - a.

A shorter, less complex version is played in New Mexico:

Víbora, víbora de la mar,
por aquí pueden pasar,
por aquí yo pasaré,
y una niña dejaré.
Una niña ¿cuál será:
la de adelante or la de atrás?

La de adelante corre más
y la de atrás se quedará.

Serpent, serpent of the sea,
they can pass through here,
I will pass through here,
and a child will remain.
A child, which will she be:
the one ahead or the one
behind?
The one ahead runs more
and the one behind is left.

VIBORA DE LA MAR
Example 2

New Mexico

1 Ví - bo- ra, ví - bo- ra. de la mar. por a- quí pue - den pa- sar,

5 por a - quí yo pa - sa - rá, y u - na ní - ña de - ja - ré.

U- na ni - ña ¿cual se - rá: la de a - de - lan - te o la de a - trás?

La de a - de - lan - te co- rre más y la de a - trás se que - da- rá

In one New Mexico version the players who form an arch have selected two items, but one of them will be the correct answer and one incorrect. When the captured player is asked to choose between the two, he is given a silly assignment (shake hands with everybody, hop on one foot, etc.) before he rejoins the serpentine line. If he answers correctly, he rejoins immediately.[81]

DE LA SIERRA MORENA

This game is included for two reasons. First it is great fun to play, suitable for all ages. But also its words have interesting correlations with songs from Spain and Mexico.

The tune from Spain, with its dark modal suggestion, is undoubtedly the oldest of the three:

POR LA SIERRA MORENA
De la Sierra Morena, Example 1

Spain

Por la sie-rra mo - re - na vie - nen ba - jan- do, vie - nen ba -

jan- do_____ dos o - ji - tos ne- gros de con - tra - ban- do. _____

The second tune is a well-known Mexican song with identical words except for the opening prepositon and the insertion of a refrain-like *cielito lindo* between phrases. Its mood, however, is completely different.

CIELITO LINDO
De la Sierra Morena, Example 2

Mexico

Finally, in the game song from New Mexico, one player stands in the center of a circle, pretending to plow or do other farm chores. The circle around him should have an even number of players. At the end of the song, after *ése es el viejo,* everyone runs to embrace another player—including *el viejo.* The person left without a partner becomes the next *viejo* as the game is repeated.

"Why are they burning the pumpkins?" someone once asked, referring to the line in the song, *se queman, se queman las calabazas.* Since this line immediately precedes the rush for partners and the inevitable partner-less player, it is likely that it has to do with the New Mexico Spanish idiom *dar las calabazas,* literally *to give the pumpkins.* When a man is interested in a woman who does not welcome his attention—or her family does not—he is "given the pumpkins." [82]

DE LA SIERRA MORENA
De la Sierra Morena, Example 3

New Mexico

CUENTOS: STORIES AND TALES

Para que enseñarle la verdad a un niño, hay que enseñarle la ficción.
In order to teach a child truth, it is necessary to teach him fiction.[83]

That the older members of the community were the tellers of tales points to the familial and community closeness which the early Hispanics in New Mexico shared in their isolation from the rest of the world. It must have been these *viejitos* who told their children the stories of the past, sometimes changing details of environment to make them more meaningful to New Mexico's children, sometimes substituting the names of saints and other religious figures for the kings and princesses and counts of the original stories. And they must have created some of their own as they went along.

The cuentos in New Mexico told by persons of Spanish speech are Spanish and came from Spain either directly or through Mexico. Here, the tales have taken on local color. Fundamentally, they are Castilian, and counterparts can be found in collections in Spain. [84]

As stated earlier, Spain was a mosaic of cultures, all of which contributed to the background from which came the missionaries, the explorers, and the early families to New Mexico. It is no surprise that Oriental tales, probably the oldest of fairy tales, as well as folk stories from other cultures had, by the sixteenth century, been assimilated into Spanish and other European folk life. This was the folktale fabric of the settlers in the New World, and these were the stories they told their children—to teach values and moral lessons, to entertain, to preserve ties to their homeland.

Religious leaders often used stories to convert and to teach the faith to the indigenous peoples they found.

Most of the tales here have direct connections to European stories, enhanced with New Mexico transmutations. A few stories found in unpublished form in the WPA Files may not be directly related to specific tales from Spain, but all are consistent with the spirit of the Spanish folktale.

LA ZORRA Y EL COYOTE (The Fox and the Coyote)

This is the familiar formula story of the animal trickster who continues to lead his more gullible friend into more and more trouble.

La Zorra, once upon a time, stole a chicken and was running through the forest hoping to find a place where she could enjoy her meal in peace, somewhere far from the dogs who had chased her from the chicken yard. It is not surprising, then, that she wasn't watching ahead as well as she might have been, and when her mortal enemy, El Coyote, suddenly appeared in her path, she forgot all about the dogs.

"Ah there, friend Zorra," El Coyote said to her as he blocked her way on the path and licked his chops. "I see you have a fine chicken. I believe I will have that for my supper."

"Oh no, please no, Coyote. I know where there are much fatter chickens, and if you will let me go on my way, you and I will go tonight and find a fine one for you."

Coyote thought this might be a very good idea, and so he agreed to it.

That night, as they came near the chicken yard, Zorra told Coyote to wait in a secret place while she stole the chicken. He trusted her, so he hid himself and waited. All at once, four barking dogs appeared and set upon Coyote, biting him viciously. Coyote ran away screaming in pain.

The fox, hiding and watching nearby, congratulated herself on her cleverness.

The next day she was lying in the sun, still pleased, thinking of the antics of the night before, when Coyote appeared.

"There you are!" he said. "Now I shall eat *you*. No more tricks from you."

"Oh no, listen!" the fox begged, "If you'll sit on this rock and scare the flies away with this stick, they'll pay us money."

"Well, all right," Coyote agreed. And Zorra ran and hid.

Coyote faithfully waved the stick back and forth, scaring the flies away—until they started to sting him! "Those are bees, not flies!" he screamed as he dashed away through the forest to escape their painful stings.

When he came upon La Zorra, who was having a hard time controlling her laughter, he was—understandably—VERY angry. "This time you are through. I'm going to eat you, and there's nothing you can do about it," Coyote told her.

"No, wait, Coyote. You can help me prepare a wedding feast for my friends if you want to. There'll be plenty to eat, and we'll have a fine time."

So El Coyote agreed to help.

"You wait here; I'll just look over the hill and see if they are coming. If you hear gunshots, it means they're on their way." And the fox rushed away, leaving her friend to watch.

Coyote waited as he'd been told. When he heard loud crackling noises, he hurried to meet the wedding party. But once again he had been deceived, for the noises were not caused by gunshots and a festive party but rather were the crackling sounds of the forest burning. To save himself, Coyote was forced to rush through the flames, severely burning his tail.

Coyote knew La Zorra was behind this, and when he found her again, he said, "You've had your last chance. I'm going to eat you right now."

"But Coyote, why would you want to eat me when I can take you to a wonderful meal of fresh fish? Come on!" the fox told him.

"All right," the trusting coyote told her, "but there had better be no more tricks."

They came to a frozen pond. Pointing to a hole in the ice, La Zorra said, "Go carefully to that hole. Sit down and put your tail in it. When you feel a bite, jerk your tail out suddenly and you'll have a fine surprise."

The coyote did as he was told, and he sat there for a very long time. When he finally tried to pull his tail up to check for fish, he was horrified to discover that his tail had frozen and dropped off.

The fox, watching from the bank, knew she had to think of something quickly. "Come on, Coyote, I've found a wonderful piece of cheese for us to share. Hurry."

El Coyote raced after La Zorra until they came to an old well. There, reflected in the water, was the full moon.

"Do you see it? Just look at that big piece of cheese!" the fox told him. "Now jump in and get it."

The coyote jumped in and he may still be there. [85]

OREJA DE BURRO Y CUERNO VERDE
(Donkey Ear and Green Horn)

In some versions of this tale it is an old woman asking for water instead of the robber hawk who effects the magic. Often--instead of the star, the ear, and the horn--beautiful things appear whenever Arcia speaks, and equally horrible things appear when the stepsisters speak.

Once there was a widower who had a beautiful daughter, Arcia. Nearby lived a widow and her two daughters. The woman was very nice, and Arcia urged her father to marry her, but he had some doubts, and at first he said:

Si hoy sopitas de miel,	If it's pudding of honey today,
mañana sopitas de hiel.	tomorrow it's pudding of gall.

Later, though, Arcia's father changed his mind and he and the woman were married, and Arcia looked forward to a happy life with her new sisters and her parents.

This was not to be. Almost immediately the sisters and the step-mother began to treat Arcia badly, perhaps because they were jealous of her beauty. When her father died, things were even worse.

One day Arcia was sent to the stream to wash *las tripitas* (intestines) of a lamb that had been killed and to bring back the day's supply of water. Just as she finished, a hawk swooped down and stole the *tripitas*. "Oh please bring them back!" she cried, as she looked up at the hawk.

He did not drop the *tripitas*, but he did drop a shining golden star which attached itself to Arcia's forehead.

She hurried home, fearful that she would be punished for losing the *tripitas*. The stepmother and her daughters were angry and were even more jealous when they saw the star on Arcia's forehead. They tried to scrub it off, but the harder they scrubbed the brighter it shone. And they certainly did not believe her story of the hawk thief.

The older stepsister decided she would go to the stream in hope she, too, would be given a star. When the hawk flew down and grabbed the *tripitas* she had just washed, she looked up and began to call him names. "Bring that back, you rotten hawk," she screamed.

He didn't bring them back, but he did drop a donkey's ear, which attached itself to her forehead.

She hurried home, frightened and crying. Her mother cut the ear, but the shorter she cut it, the longer it grew.

The other stepsister thought she would do a better job, so she went to the stream to wash *tripitas*. The hawk came and stole them, and as she was screaming at him, he dropped a green horn, which attached itself to her forehead. When she got home, her mother tried to file it off, but it grew longer and longer.

Soon after this, the prince gave a ball. He invited all the young women of the kingdom because he was looking for one to be his wife. Both Oreja de Burro and Cuerno Verde covered their forehead attachments, dressed in their finest, and went to the ball. Of course, Arcia was not permitted to go, but she did slip away to look into the window at the gala ball.

While she was looking through the window, her star attracted the attention of the prince, and he ran outside to find her, for she was the most beautiful girl he had ever seen. "That is the girl I will marry," he said. But Arcia was nowhere to be found.

The next day he began his search, stopping at every house to see the women who lived there, always asking about the girl with the star on her forehead.

"Have you seen her?" he asked Oreja de Burro and Cuerno Verde. "Of course not," they told him.

He was about to leave, when it seemed the cat was speaking to him:

Miáu, miáu,	Meow, meow,
Arcia atrás de la	Arcia is behind
artesa está.	the chest.

And this was the way in which the prince found Arcia. A great wedding feast was planned, and Arcia became the bride of the prince.[86]

-59-

LOS TRES CONSEJOS (The Three Pieces of Advice)

Perhaps a moral to this story can be found in the realization that sometimes we are given advice that appears irrelevant at the time, but that later proves to be very valuable.

Once upon a time, when there was great distress in the land, a poor man was forced to leave his wife and children and go out into the world to earn a living. He found a place where he could work for a farmer if he promised to stay three years, collecting his wages at the end of that time.

When the three years had passed and he asked for his wages, the farmer told him he could choose between three heavy sacks of silver or three pieces of advice that would serve him well all his life. The poor man, not knowing how he could carry the heavy sacks home anyway, chose the three pieces of advice.

"First," the farmer told him, "never leave the main road for a trail; second, never ask about something that does not concern you; and finally, pay no attention to gossip." The man thanked the farmer and set off for his home.

He had hardly started on the road when he met two men who wanted to go along with him and who told him, "We know a shortcut, a trail that will save many miles." Although he was eager to get home as quickly as possible, the man remembered his first piece of advice, never leave the main road for a trail, so he thanked them and continued on the main road. Sure enough, he found out later, the two men who took the trail were set upon by robbers, and all their belongings were stolen.

Soon he came to an inn where he asked for food. The owner invited him to sit at the table and brought him a plate on which was served the head of a man. Of course he wanted to ask questions, but he remembered the second piece of advice, never ask about something that does not concern you. So when the innkeeper asked him what he thought of the head, he replied simply, "It's a good head."

"Have you no questions?" the innkeeper asked.

"Oh no, *señor.*"

"Very well," the innkeeper replied, "I would have made you my next victim if you had asked questions as all the others did, but since you did not, you may continue on your way."

The man was relieved and hurried on the road toward his home. Just as he was coming into the town where he and his family had lived, he met an old friend. "I'm glad to see you," he said, "and I will be so happy to see my wife and children."

"Oh, but hadn't you heard?" his old friend asked. "She thought you were not coming back, so she has married another."

The man was very sad and started to go back toward the farm where he had worked for three years. But then he remembered the third piece of advice, pay no attention to gossip, so he turned back and went on to his home where he had left his wife and children. To his great joy he found them waiting eagerly for his arrival.[87]

CUENTOS DE DON CACAHUATE

Bertoldo and Pedro Urdimales are rogues from Spain who appear in New Mexican tales, Bertoldo as a comic figure in Los Pastores, and Pedro in a large number of stories. Other New Mexico pícaros include Juan Tonto, Juan Bobo, El Pelón, Juan Catorce, and our friend here, Don Cacahuate. Part of the humor of the Cacahuate stories is in the names of some of the characters: Cacahuate=Peanut; Cebolla=Onion; Sr. Sabelotodo=Mr. Know-it-all; Orejas de Burro=Ears of the donkey.

Don Cacahuate was born in Santa Rosa de Lima on the Chama River sometime before 1750, though no one is quite sure when. We know he was invited to go along on the Escalante expedition in 1776. Unfortunately, he couldn't go because he had a bad cold. And apparently, he is still alive and well. Once, a long time ago, he and his son Bavitas were en route from Abiquiu to Española. It was a long journey, and they stopped to spend the night at Arroyo del Oso, where they saw a wagon and a team of horses stuck in the mud. They were investigating it when Cacahuate's cousin, Señor Pedro de Urdimales, approached from the other side of the wagon. A loud argument soon broke out concerning the color of the wagon. Cacahuate insisted it was red, Pedro was just as sure it was blue. Bavitas, seeing no other way to calm the shouting men, struck one of the horses under the tail, causing it to surge forward, pulling the wagon from the mud. As the horses ran away, the two men realized the wagon was red on one side and blue on the other side.

Cacahuate's father was Señor Reñegitos. When the younger man fell in love with a girl, he and his father went to the girl's father to ask for her hand. The girl's father, Señor Sabelotodo, was astounded at the request. "Why this girl?" he asked, "she is ugly, fat, short, and you are a man of high status. I don't know why you want her." "Sir," Cacahuate replied, "is it not enough that I choose her to be my wife?" And so *no le dieron calabazas* (they didn't give him the pumpkins).[88] Cacahuate and his father went to talk to the priest, Father Juan Jose Toledo, about arrangements for the wedding. When they found that a *misa cantada* (sung mass) cost $10 and a *misa resada* (spoken mass) cost $5, they arranged for a *misa chiflada* (whistled mass) at a price in the middle.

Cacahuate had a donkey, Orejas de Burro. Once when Cacahuate was chasing him, the donkey ran into the town, stopping just outside the door of a cantina. Two *médios borrachos* (men half drunk) came out and tried to help, but the donkey eluded them and dashed into the cantina. Startled, three *señoritas* sitting in the cantina screamed. In turn the donkey was frightened and, trying to escape, stepped into a metal spittoon and was unable to release his foot. He raced out and away, and has never been seen again, though he is often heard at night, clanking along in the arroyos. And one person is pretty sure he saw La Llorona riding him.

Cacahuate's horse, Palo Verde, had a fancy gait. As he trotted over the cobblestone streets, he was pleased with the attention he got because his footsteps seemed to say, "Za-ca-TE-cas, Za-ca-TE-cas, Za-ca-TE-cas." Once, as he was trotting around the plaza with Cacahuate on his back, a bolt of lightning struck and broke Palo Verde in half. Cacahuate knew something was wrong when he heard only, "Za-ca, Za-ca, Za-ca." So he looked back, saw the rear half of Palo Verde behind them, and waited for it to catch up, "TE-cas, TE-cas, TE-cas." Then they went on, "Za-ca-TE-cas, Za-ca-TE-cas, Za-ca-TE-cas."

Once, when Cacahuate went hunting, he took along a bag of peaches. When a deer appeared in front of him, he quickly loaded his gun and fired. (Unfortunately, he had no ammunition, but he was sure a peach pit would serve.) The deer fell, but it got up and ran away before Cacahuate could get to it. Several years later when he was hunting again, he saw a peach tree loaded with fruit. He climbed up to get a few peaches, but suddenly, with Cacahuate at its top, the tree began running through the forest. Sure enough, that peach seed had begun growing in the deer's head.

Don Cacahuate and his wife, Doña Cebolla, were poor most of the time. Once, when they had nothing at all in the house to eat or drink, Cacahuate asked his wife to bring him a cup of coffee. " *Como?*"(how?) she asked in disgust. "*Con azúcar; tu sabes como me gusta el café*" (with sugar; you know how I like my coffee), her husband answered.

It may have been Don Cacahuate and his cousin Pedro Urdimales who made a promise to *el Señor* to make a pilgrimage, perhaps to *el Santuario*, with beans in their shoes. It was a long walk, and hard. Pedro was in great discomfort, and he wondered why Cacahuate seemed to have no problem. "I promised to walk with beans in my shoes," Cacahuate said, "but I didn't promise not to cook them."[89]

CUENTOS DE TOMASITO

Tomasito is new Mexico's answer to Tom Thumb. He is very small but very great in achievement and kindness. He is something of a mixture between a Spanish santo and an Indian "littleman," a fetish carried in the hair for advice in emergencies.

Once Tomasito was hiding in the tail of a burro he loved very much. His master was trying to sell the burro so that he would not have to gather and haul firewood for his wife every year. A buyer was about to make a deal, and Tomasito tried desperately to think of a way to make the buyer just go away and not take the burro. So he pulled a hair from the burro's tail. The burro kicked violently, almost hitting the prospective buyer, who became rather angry. This had worked so well that Tomasito tried it again and again, with the burro responding as expected each time. The disgusted buyer backed out of the deal and went away. Now his master has no excuse not to gather firewood for his wife.

Tomasito hated not doing what everybody else did, so he went on a buffalo hunt with his friends. He came upon a buffalo and attacked it as high as he could reach with his spear—slightly above the right front ankle. The buffalo thought a bee had stung him, and he swallowed Tomasito. At first our little hero was frightened, but he soon calmed down when he realized he could have fresh buffalo liver every day, as well as a nice, dark, warm place to live. Meantime the hunters looked for him in all the coyote holes and wherever they could think he might be. They went home sadly without him. The next year, however, they killed that very buffalo and were shocked when Tomasito jumped out, angry, sputtering, "You have ruined my house, spoiled my living." Everyone was happy Tomasito was found. When they got back to the village, a great feast was prepared. Tomasito drank too much wine, almost half a thimbleful, and he began to brag about his bravery. But he never went hunting again. He spends his time now spearing cockroaches in his mother's kitchen.[90]

NO CALAMITY LIKE A BAD NEIGHBOR

San Isidro and Santa Rita were bean and chile growers. On May 15, San Isidro Day, Isidro was plowing with his oxen when an angel appeared and told him God didn't like him to plow on a feast day. Isidro replied he was sorry, but he had to; the season was late and his plants weren't in. The angel warned him that hail would come and destroy his plants if he didn't obey God, but Isidro said he would make the best of the hail. The angel left, and Isidro continued his plowing.

Then a second angel appeared, delivering the same message from

God. Isidro, a little irritated by this time, said he didn't care if it was a day for all the saints; he was going to keep right on plowing. The angel warned that God would send grasshoppers and worms to eat his plants, but Isidro said he was going to continue plowing and that he would make the best of the grasshoppers and worms. And he added, "Tell God I'd be pleased not to be annoyed by any more young angels." Surely they could find something better to do, he thought. And the angel left.

A third angel came, repeated the request, and threatened Isidro that God would send him a bad neighbor if he didn't stop his plowing. Isidro said, "All right. Tell God He wins. To have a bad neighbor is too hard to bear even for a saint."[91]

LAS TRES VIEJAS (The Three Old Women)

Once, there were three old women. The oldest had become a burden on the other two, and they decided to do something about it. So they stuffed her up a bit, dressed her in nice clothes, and placed her outside where the King would be sure to see her when he rode by. "She is beautiful," the King thought, "I will marry her." And so he had her brought to the castle and ordered the royal seamstresses to make a fine dress for her. When they began to fit her, the seamstresses discovered she was not a beautiful young girl, but an old woman. When they told the King, he was both angry and disappointed, and he said, "Throw her out!"

They took him at his literal word and threw her out the window. She fell into a tree, got caught in a branch, and there she hung. Three witches flew by, singing:

Lunes, martes, miércoles, tres;	Monday, Tuesday, Wednesday, three;
jueves, viernes, sábado, seis.	Thursday, Friday, Saturday, six.

As they flew by, the old woman screamed out:

y domingo siete.	and Sunday seven.

This startled the witches, who flew back to investigate. When they heard her story, they decided to help her, so they threw her into a nearby lake, and when she emerged, she was a beautiful, seventeen-year-old girl.

Again the King saw her, fell in love, and, this time, married her.

Now the two old women who had started this whole affair came to see her. They were very jealous and asked her how she had achieved this beauty and youth, which had led to her new life of luxury.

"Easy," she told them, "just shave off all your skin."

And so one of the old women hired a boy to shave off her skin. She died, of course. And the third old woman decided to stay as she was.[92]

When a poor couple had a son, they asked their wealthy neighbors to be *padrinos* (godparents), thinking this would inspire a handsome gift to the baby. The *padrinos* came to the baptismal party and had a good time. When they left, they said, "Thank you, *compadres*, for the honor you have conferred upon us by permitting us to be your baby's *padrinos*, thus becoming your *compadres*. You are the very best of neighbors."

But no gift! The parents were distressed at the godparents' stinginess.

The young mother thought and thought. Finally she came up with the idea of stealing the horse their neighbors loved very much. "Get it," she told her husband, "find a place to hide it, tie it up, and I'll tell you what to do next."

After the horse was stolen, she went to visit the neighbors, expressing her sympathy for their loss. "Yes," the rich neighbor said, "I would give $100 to get that horse back."

"Well," said she, "maybe my husband can help. He is a diviner, you know." And so it was arranged that the young man would divine the location of the horse. The couple drew a map with many turnbacks and crossings and took it to their neighbor. "Here you will find your treasure," they told their neighbor. He sent his servants out immediately to retrieve the horse, and indeed, there it was, just where the couple had said it would be. So the owner had a wonderful party and gave his younger neighbor $100.

Word spread fast throughout the kingdom. When the Princess lost her ring, the King called for the young diviner. The poor man was horrified. He said to his wife, "What a fix you've gotten me into! What can I do?" But the wife had no answer.

So the man went before the King, who promised him $200 if he found the ring--and execution in three days if he didn't. The poor frightened man was placed in a room alone, to be tended by three guards.

The next morning the first guard brought his breakfast, and the young man said, "Thanks be to God, of three I have seen one." The guard was very frightened and he called the other two guards together for a discussion.

"What shall we do?" they asked each other. "He knows! Perhaps we should offer him $100 if he promises not to tell the King we stole the ring."

And so they confessed to their prisoner that they were the thieves and offered him the money. The young man agreed to their conditions and began to plan a way for his own release.

"Put the ring in the corn which you feed to the turkeys; then watch to see which turkey eats the ring," he told them.

They followed his directions carefully and reported back to him that the grayest turkey in the flock had eaten the ring.

On the third day he was once again brought before the King. The young man told the King the grayest turkey of the flock should be killed. This done, the ring was found, the young man collected $100 from the dishonest guards and $200 from the King, and he left for a far country. No one has heard from him since.[93]

GRISELDA

Griselda was a beautiful and kind girl who spent her days caring for her father and her sheep. One day, a deer was wounded by the King and his hunting party. The deer ran to Griselda.

The King and his party, following the deer, came upon Griselda and were astounded at her beauty.

"Are you from this world or another?" he asked.

"From this world."

"Will you marry me?"

"No," she told him.

"But why not?"

"Because you are of royal blood and I am not."

The King went home, disappointed, but he ordered a beautiful dress to be made for Griselda. Word spread that the King wanted to get married. The villagers prepared for the royal feast. Everyone followed in the procession, wondering whom the King would choose. They were surprised when he turned into the forest.

He stopped before Griselda's father, Janiculo, who was sitting outside smoking his pipe.

The King told Janiculo he wanted to marry Griselda, but Janiculo replied that no such thing should happen because the King would later regret that his wife was not of royal blood.

Finally, though, after persuasion by the King, the old man agreed to the marriage. The King promised he would always love her and care for her. But Griselda was still reluctant. Nonetheless, they were married and celebrated in a wedding feast that lasted three days.

About a year later, they had a baby girl. When the child was one year old, the King told Griselda the people of his kingdom were growing mutinous because the baby was not of royal blood. "They will kill the child or me," he told his wife.

"Then let them kill the child," she answered sadly.

The King put the baby in a carriage and sent her to his sister, who was sworn to secrecy. "Keep her and raise her as befits a princess," he told his sister.

After another year they had a baby boy. And again, the King told his wife the people were mutinous and had threatened to kill him or the baby.

Again, the Queen agreed that the baby should be killed. The King sent the child to his sister, saying, "Raise him as befits a prince."

Seventeen years later, the King told his wife that his mutinous people demanded that he get rid of her. She agreed this was best and went home to her father. But very shortly, she was called back to supervise the renovation of the palace for the King's new bride.

Soon after she returned to the palace, a carriage arrived in which there were, with the King, a young man and woman and an old woman.

"That beautiful young woman must be the King's new bride," Griselda thought, and she said to the King, "You have chosen well. Your new bride is indeed of royal blood, your Majesty, your equal."

Then the King told her everything and assured her that there could never be any other Queen but Griselda herself. And the King and Queen, their children, and his sister lived together happily for a very long time.[94]

PUSO UNO; PUSO DOS; PUSO TRES; PUSO CUATRO
(She Laid One..Two..Three..Four)

La gallina pupujada	The ruffled hen
puso un huevo en la arada,	laid an egg in the furrow
puso uno,	she laid one,
puso dos,	she laid two,
puso tres...[95]	she laid three...

There was once, many years ago, a little hen named Carmen who lived alone in her small *gallinero* (henhouse). She was lonely and looked forward to the time her four eggs would hatch so she would have *pollitas* (chicks) to keep her company.

After two weeks, Carmen grew tired of sitting on her nest and went out to clean her patio. She had hardly started when she heard something from inside the *gallinero*. She rushed back in and saw that one of the eggs had cracked and her first *pollita* had been born.

" ¡Mi hija!" she cried. "Welcome to the world! I am going to call you Estella because you are like a beautiful little star."

Just then another egg cracked, and out stepped another *pollita*!

"Mama, is that my sister?" Estella asked.

"Yes, it is, and I'm going to name her Rafaelita because she is like a little angel. Now, you come with me, Estella, and help clean the patio. We'll leave Rafaelita here to rest a little while."

As soon as Carmen and Estella left the *gallinero*, little Rafaelita picked up one of the eggs still in the nest and threw it as hard as she could to the floor!

"Oh Mama, come quick!" Rafaelita was very frightened at what she had done.

When Carmen and Estella rushed in, they watched excitedly as another tiny chick brushed the shell from its back.

" ¡Mi pollita! Are you all right?"

"Yes," the newest chick said, "but who are you and where am I?"

"I'm your mama, these are your sisters, and you're in your home. And I am going to name you Suertuda because you are very lucky that you were not hurt."

In that moment, as Carmen and her three daughters spoke, the fourth egg cracked open. The four stared in amazement.

"Mama, is that my sister?" Estella asked.

"But Mama, why doesn't she look like us?" Rafaelita asked.

"Well Mama, I think she doesn't have the same papa as ours," Suertuda added.

"Yes, she does," Carmen told the girls, "it's just that she looks like your grandfather."

"Who are all of you?" the new *pollita* asked.

"We are your family, *mi hija*, and I'm going to name you *La Gallinita Pinta*" (the little spotted hen).

"What a strange name. Why are you calling me that?"

"Because you are white with black circles. But enough of this talk, girls. You must all make your nests and begin to lay eggs."

And this they set out to do, all of them except *la Pintita*.

"I believe she is ill," the mother said.

"She can't lay eggs, Mama, because she is of two colors," Estella said.

"No, no. She just doesn't want to lay," Rafaelita added.

"You're all wrong," said Suertuda. "She doesn't lay because she is too little and doesn't know how."

"Mama," Pintita broke in, "I am ready to lay eggs, but I need a plow."

"A plow!" they gasped.

But Carmen quickly brought her a plow.

"Now," said Pintita, "please don't look at me, but come back in an hour and see if I can lay eggs."

So they left her with her plow. When an hour had passed, they returned.

There sat Pintita. "You thought I couldn't lay eggs? Here they are: ten eggs! Count them yourselves!"

And they all began to count: "puso uno; puso dos; puso tres; puso cuatro; puso cinco; puso seis; puso siete; puso ocho; puso nueve; puso diez."

"Now." La Pintita said, "all of you run along and play. I am going to lay more eggs."[96]

NOTES AND SOURCES

1. Roberto Mondragon, Rio Grande *Sun*, April 18, 1991.
2. Rubén Cobos, collector and translator, *Refranes: Southwestern Proverbs* (Santa Fe: Museum of New Mexico Press, 1985).
3. Carl Orff, "Orff-Schulwerk: Past and Future," *Orff Re-Echoes*, Isabel Carley, ed. (American Orff -Schulwerk Association, 1977), 9.
4. Jose Manuel Gomez-Tabanera, ed., *El Folklore Español* (Madrid: Instituto Español de Antropología Aplicada, 1968), Preface.
5. I first heard this from Corinne Trujillo, Alcalde. Since then a number of others—once reminded—remembered it as a rhyme from their own childhood.
6. Mary Helen Fierro Klare, Los Alamos, remembers this teasing rhyme from her childhood in El Paso. It is also to be found in *A Dictionary of New Mexico and Southern Colorado Spanish*, Rubén Cobos, editor (Santa Fe: Museum of New Mexico Press, 1984), 167.
7. Roberto Mondragon, quoting Maria Luisa Ponce in *Rimas Infantiles*, Rio Grande *Sun*, June 6, 1991.
8. Mrs. Emilio A. Pacheco, reporter, collected by Manuel Berg, September 1937, WPA Files #165. Archives of New Mexico, State Records Center, Santa Fe.

In 1935, as a partial answer to widespread unemployment and an alternative to welfare, the Works Progress Administration was begun. This federal agency, taking different forms in different parts of the country, provided employment for craftsmen in all the arts. Of special interest in the preservation of folklore in New Mexico were the Federal Music Project and the Federal Writers' Project, later reorganized as the Writers' Program. Workers in both these programs were assigned the task of collecting folk materials from New Mexicans. In an article in the Las Vegas *Optic*, February 12, 1937, Music Project Director Helen Chandler Ryan is quoted, "The fact that New Mexico has such a rich heritage of Hispanic-American folklore, which for lack of recording is being lost to present and future generations, has prompted the setting up of folklore collecting and singing projects...to help preserve almost forgotten tunes and verses for posterity." Writers pursued the collection of stories, proverbs, rhymes, games, plays, beliefs and superstitions. Today most of the original material collected during the WPA years, 1935-1943, is preserved in the archives of the State Records Center and the Palace of the Governors Historical Library in Santa Fe. Scholars and writers on Southwest folkloric subjects have worked with this material, and their works are included in the Bibliography, but much of the material in the collections remains unpublished.

9. Aurelio M. Espinosa, *The Folklore of Spain in the American Southwest: Traditional Spanish Folk Literature in Northern New Mexico and Southern Colorado*, J. Manuel Espinosa, ed. (Norman: University of Oklahoma Press, 1979).
10. Ibid.
11. Teresa Trujillo, Los Alamos, shared this verse remembered from her childhood in Taos.
12. John O. West, *Mexican-American Folklore: Legends, Songs, Festivals, Proverbs, Crafts, Tales of Saints, of Revolutionaries, and More* (Little Rock: August House, 1988).

13. Ofelia Neri was a student in a music education class I taught at California State University, Chico, in 1989. During the semester she shared a number of songs and rhymes which she remembered from her childhood in Los Angeles. This was one of them.

14. Charles Aranda, collector and translator, *Dichos: Proverbs and Sayings from the Spanish* (Santa Fe: Sunstone Press, 1975).

15. Arthur L. Campa, *Hispanic Culture in the Southwest* (Norman: University of Oklahoma Press, 1979), 234.

16. Aurora Lucero-White Lea, gatherer and interpreter, *Literary Folklore of the Hispanic Southwest* (San Antonio: The Naylor Company, 1953), 123.

17. Bonifacio Gil García, *Cancionero de Extremadura*, Tomo I (Badajoz, Spain: Imprenta de la Excma. Diputación, 1961), 89.

18. The version here is essentially the one collected by Lea (op. cit.), but the lines concerning Don Gato's burial were incomplete, so the gap is filled here by a version from Santa Cruz—though some of the other words in this second version were slightly different from Lea's. Campa (op. cit.), found the poem in Mora County almost identical to the version cited here, curiously enough with parts of the same lines missing. The Mora version also adds a final line not found in other versions: *A lo español y francés, lo que le luce al soldado.* Another version collected by Campa in Doña Ana County, probably more closely related to Mexican sources than to Spanish, retains the story but tells it in different words:

Estaba Señor don Gato en silla de oro sentado
con camisita de lino y zapatito bordado.
Entró su compadre y dijo que si quería ser casado
con una gato por ver la pronto se echó del tejado abajo;
se ha rompido tres costillas y se ha lastimado un brazo.
Que vengan, que vengan todos los médicos cirujanos,
y que venga entre todos ellos el médico don Carlo.
Los ratones de alegría se visten de colorado,
las gatas de luto negro, y los gatitos:—miau, miau.

19. John Donald Robb, *Hispanic Folk Music of New Mexico and the Southwest: A Self Portrait of a People* (Norman: University of Oklahoma Press, 1980).

20. Emilio Gonzalez Barroso, *Cancionero Popular Extremeño: Recopilación, adaptaciones, indicativo de tonalidades, transposición musical y comentarios* (Badajoz, Spain: Biblioteca Básica Extremeña, Universitas Editorial, 1985). Gonzalez cites Gil García (Tomo I, op. cit.), as an earlier collector of this *nana.*

21. Alvaro Fernaud Palarea, ed., *Cuadernos de Cultura Popular: Melodias Tradicionales para Uso Escolar* (Caracas, Venezuela: Consejo Nacional de la Cultura Conac, 1988).

22. Bonifacio Gil García, *Cancionero de Extremadura*, Tomo II (Badajoz, Spain: Imprenta de la Excma. Diputación, 1956), 85.

23. *Canciones para la Juventud de America*, compiladas por la Facultad de Ciencias y Artes Musicales de la Universidad de Chile y la Asociación de Educación Musical de Chile, Volume II (Washington: Unión Panamericana, Secretaría General, Organización de los Estados Americános, 1960).

24. Vioma Selph in *Compendio de Folklore Nuevo Mejicano—Conjunto de las Tradiciones, Creencias y Costumbres Populares* (Santa Fe: La Sociedad

Folklorica de Santa Fe, Nuevo Mejico, n. d.). Ofelia Neri reports this variant:

> A la rurru niño,
> a la rurru ya,
> duérmase mi niño,
> duérmase ya,
> si no viene el coco
> y se lo comerá.

25. Jose and Pedro Gurule, reporters, collected by Lou Sage Batchen, Las Placitas, WPA Files 5-5-47 #46, December 1940. Palace of the Governors Historical Library, Santa Fe. See also Espinosa, op. cit.

26. Roger Caillois, quoted by Sergio Hernández de Soto in *Juegos Infantiles de Extremadura* (Jerez de la Frontera: Editora de Extremadura, 1988), 7.

27. Michel de Montaigne, quoted in *The Oxford Dictionary of Quotations*, Third Edition (Oxford, New York, Toronto, Melbourne: Oxford University Press, 1980), 354.

28. Sergio Hernández de Soto, *Juegos Infantiles de Extremadura*, op. cit.

29. Phyllis S. Weikart, *Round the Circle: Key Experiences in Movement for Children* (Ypsilanti: High/Scope Press, 1987).

30. This little game came into my collection quite by accident: I had asked my son-in-law, VIctor Apodaca, raised in Santa Fe but living now in Taos, if he could remember any games from his childhood. He told me, honestly I think, that he could not. Later that same day I heard him playing this game with his baby.

31. Vioma Selph, op. cit.

32. Cobos, *A Dictionary of New Mexico and Southern Colorado Spanish*, op. cit., 97.

33. Espinosa, op. cit.

34. West, op. cit.

35. Hernández de Soto, op. cit.

36. Gil García, Tomo II, op. cit.

37. Hernández de Soto, op. cit.

38. West, op. cit.

39. Ibid.

40. Hernández de Soto, op. cit.

41. Cobos, *A Dictionary of New Mexico and Southern Colorado Spanish*, op. cit., 41.

42. West, op. cit.

43. Ibid. See also Espinosa who finds a similar rhyme both in Galicia, Spain, and in New Mexico:

> Éste es el chiquito y bonito.
> Éste es el señor de los anillos.
> Éste es el largo y vano.
> Éste es el chupa cazuelas.
> Éste es el mata venados.

44. Hernández de Soto, op. cit.

45. Espinosa, op. cit. See also Vicente Mendoza, *Lirica Infantil de Mexico* (El Colegio de Mexico, 1951) who collected this variant :

> Aserrín asserán,
> los maderos de San Juan
> piden pan y no les dan
> riqui riqui riquirrán.

46. West, op. cit. See also WPA Files #171, Lorin Brown; WPA Files #145, Manuel Berg collected from Cleofas Monreal, Archives of New Mexico, State Records Center, Santa Fe. See also Mendoza, op. cit.:

Riquerrán riquerrán
los maderos de San Juan
piden pan y no se lo dan
piden queso y les dan un hueso
para que se rasquen
ese pescuezo.

47. Hernández de Soto, op. cit.

48. Lorin Brown, collector, WPA Files #171. Archives of New Mexico, State Records Center, Santa Fe.

49. Eugene. F. Ulibarri, collector, WPA Files #573. Archives of New Mexico, State Records Center, Santa Fe.

50. Espinosa, op. cit.

51. Cobos, *A Dictionary of New Mexico and Southern Colorado Spanish*, op. cit.

52. Manuel Vizuete Carrizosa and Juan Gutierrez Casala, *Juegos Populares Extremeños* (Salamanca, Spain: Consejeria de Education y Cultura, 1986), 24.

53. Ibid.

54. Anonymous, "Life and Play of the Children," WPA Files 5-5-49, #42. Palace of the Governors Historical Library, Santa Fe.

55. Ibid.

56. Reyes N. Martinez, collector, WPA Files #490. Archives of New Mexico, State Records Center, Santa Fe.

57. Lorin Brown, collector, WPA Files #214, Archives of New Mexico, State Records Center, Santa Fe.

58. Aurelio Martinez, reporter, collected by Reyes N. Martinez, WPA Files #466. Archives of New Mexico, State Records Center, Santa Fe.

59. Lorin Brown, collector, WPA Files. Archives of New Mexico, State Records Center, Santa Fe.

60. Cobos, *A Dictionary of New Mexico and Southern Colorado Spanish*, 39.

61. This and other children's games are to be found in the following WPA Files in the Archives of New Mexico, State Records Center, Santa Fe: 2, 7, 9, 24, 25, 26, 27, 28, 56, 148, 197, 48, 199, 214, 222, 341, 343, 355, 382, 388, 400, 402, 407, 419, 444, 458, 465, 466, 488, 490, 573, 576.

62. Vizuete Carrizosa and Gutierrez Casala, op. cit., 24.

63. Ibid.

64. Anonymous, WPA Files #2. Archives of New Mexico, State Records Center, Santa Fe.

65. Richard B. Stark, ed., *Juegos Infantiles Cantados en Nuevo Mexico* (Santa Fe: Museum of New Mexico Press, 1973). This version is also used in many parts of Mexico and Latin America.

66. Louisa Martinez, Arroyo Hondo, WPA Files #341. Archives of New Mexico, State Records Center, Santa Fe.

67. Vizuete Carrizosa and Gutierrez Casala, op. cit.

68. An historically interesting booklet, *Juegos y Juguetes de Nuevo Mexico*, Hispanic Cultural Heritage Project of the Museum of New Mexico (n. d.), contains this song as well as some of the others included in this book.

69. Hernández de Soto, op. cit.

70. Anjelica Perez was my student in a music education class at California State University, Chico, in 1989. She provided many childhood games, this being one, which she and her family had known in Michoacán, Mexico.

71. Stark, op. cit.

72. Lorin W. Brown with Charles L. Briggs and Marta Weigle, *Hispano Folklife of New Mexico, The Lorin W. Brown Federal Writers Project Manuscripts* (Albuquerque: University of New Mexico Press, 1978).

73. Aurelio Armendaris, collector, WPA Files #28. Archives of New Mexico, State Records Center, Santa Fe.

74. Gil García, op. cit.

75. Brown, op. cit.

76. Gil, Tomo II, op. cit.

77. Reyes N. Martinez, collector, WPA Files #382. Archives of New Mexico, State Records Center, Santa Fe.

78. Brown, op. cit. See also Note 61.

79. Anonymous, WPA Games Files, see Note 61.

80. Anjelica Perez.

81. Stark, op. cit.

82. I learned this game a number of years ago from Jenny Vincent, folk musician from San Cristobal. I have since seen it written in a collection of Spanish songs and dances produced by the music departments of the Albuquerque Public Schools and the University of New Mexico, *Musica de Nuevo Mexico para Cantar y Bailar.* Here too it is credited to Mrs. Vincent.

83. Credited to Plato.

84. Lucero-White Lea, op. cit., 154.

85. This story, with many variations in details but always the same in outcome, is popular in Spanish folk literature. It can be found in collections of many of the authors listed in the Bibliography, including Rael, West, Lea, Campa, Espinosa, and others.

86. See Note 85. This story is also known as *Maria la Fea y Maria la Bonita* and *Estrella de Oro.* In still another version, contributed by Ezequiel Lucero of Las Vegas, the heroine's name is Granito de Oro.

87. Reyes N. Martinez, collector, WPA Files #482. Archives of New Mexico, State Records Center, Santa Fe. Also see Note 85.

88. *Dar calabazas una mujer a un hombre,* to reject a man's proposal of marriage. Se also Note 82.

89. Gilberto Benito Cordova, *Abiquiu and Don Cacahuate: A Folk History of a New Mexican Village* (Los Cerrillos: San Marcos Press, 1973). Some of these stories can be found in West, op. cit.

90. Genevieve Chapin, collector, WPA Files #134. Archives of New Mexico, State Records Center, Santa Fe.

91. Ibid., #134 Exp. #14.

92. Guadalupe Gallegos, reported, collected by Bright Lynn, WPA Files 5-5-6 #13. Palace of the Governors Historical Library, Santa Fe.

93. Florentine Baca, reported, collected by Simeon Rejada, translated by Lorin Brown, February 1939, WPA Files #153. Archives of New Mexico, State Records Center, Santa Fe.

94. Guadalupe Gallegos, reporter, collected by Bright Lynn, Las Vegas, November 1933, WPA Files 5-5-6, #2. Palace of the Governors Historical Library, Santa Fe.

95. Brown, op. cit.

96. Lisa Archuleta, Berlinda Herrera, Rosella Montoya, Gloria Ortega, Julie Ann Pacheco y Patsy Tafoya, *El Crepúsculo*, Taos *News*, February 16, 1989, A12. This strange little story was reported by a group of Headstart teachers whose purpose was to preserve the old lore. A *verso* from Extremadura may be related:

> La gallina Pupujá
> pone huevos en el corral,
> pone uno, pone dos,
> pone tres, pone cuatro,
> pone cinco, pone seis,
> pone siete, pone ocho.
> Tapa biscocho.

SOURCES OF MUSIC EXAMPLES

Las Canciones

El Señor Don Gato
page 14:

Example 1: Bonifacio Gil García, *Cancionero de Extremadura*, Tomo II (Badajoz, Spain: Imprenta de la Excma. Diputación, 1954), 79.

Example 2: Kurt Schindler, *Folk Music and Poetry of Spain and Portugal* (New York: Hispanic Institute, 1941), #695.

page 15:

Example 3: Bonifacio Gil García, *Cancionero de Extremadura*, Tomo I, second edition (Badajoz, Spain: Imprenta de la Excma. Diputación, 1961), 86.

Example 4: Schindler, op. cit., #802.

page 16:

Example 5: John Donald Robb, *Hispanic Folk Music of New Mexico and the Southwest: A Self-Portrait of a People* (Norman: University of Oklahoma Press, 1980), 84.

A la Puerta del Cielo
page 17:

Example 1: Emilio Gonzalez Barroso, *Cancionero Popular Extremeño* (Badajoz, Spain: Biblioteca Basica Extremeña, 1985), 95.

Example 2: Schindler, op. cit., #721.

page 18:

Example 3: Alvaro Fernaud Palarea, ed., *Cuadernos de Cultura Popular: Melodias Tradicionales Para Uso Escolar* (Caracas, Venezuela: Consejo Nacional de la Cultura Conac,1988), 11.

Example 4: I have "always" known this song. I was told—as early as the 1940's—that it was indigenous to New Mexico. I do not know that that is true or that it is not true. I have not heard it sung by traditional Spanish folksingers in New Mexico.

Songs of El Coco
page 19:

Example 1: Gil Tomo II, op. cit., 71.

page 20:

Example 2: Schindler, op. cit., #371.

page 21:

Example 3: Schindler, op. cit.

Example 4: Gil, Tomo II, op. cit., # 152.

Example 5: Manuel García-Matos, *Cancionero Popular de la Provincia de Cáceres* (Barcelona: Consejo Superior de Investigaciones Científicas Instituto Español de Musicología, Consejería de Cultura de la Junta Regional de Extremadura, 1982), 27.

Example 6: Gil, Tomo I, op. cit.

Los Juegos

Musical notation for all the singing games—excepting that found in cancioneros from Spain—is readily available in a number of sources, though I know of no single source that includes notation for all of them. Sources listed here—again excepting those from Spain—are simply representative of available published materials. Melodies have been transposed in some cases.

Matarile
page 38:
Example 1: widely known traditional tune.
page 40:
Example 2: Richard B. Stark, compiler, *Juegos Infantiles Cantados en Nuevo México* (Santa Fe: Museum of New Mexico Press, 1973).
Example 3: José Posada-Charrúa, Hiltraud Reckmann, Mary Shamrock, eds. *Games and Songs of Mexico* (Redwood City, CA: Friedel Musikalien Haus, 1990), 23.
page 41:
Example 4: Dolores Gonzáles, ed., *Canciones y Juegos de Nuevo Mexico* (New York: Barnes, 1974).

Juan Pirulero
page 42:
Juegos y Juguetes de Nuevo Mexico, Hispanic Cultural Heritage Project, Museum of New Mexico, no date.

La Rueda de San Miguel
page 43:
Juegos y Juguetes de Nuevo Mexico, op. cit.

El Burrito
page 45:
Example 1: Stark, op. cit.
Example 2: Gil García, Tomo II, 76.

La Viudita de Santa Isabel
page 47:
Gonzales, op. cit.

El Florón
page 48:
Example 1: Gil García, Tomo II, op. cit. , 66.
page 49:
Example 2: Stark, op. cit.
Example 3: Jim Ryan, ed., Chiquitos: *Hispanic and English Songs with Orff Instruments, Games and Dances for Pre-K through First Grade* (Leon Valley, TX: Brain Dance, Ink, 1990).

Hilitos de Oro
page 51:
> Gonzéles, op. cit.

Víbora de la Mar
page 53:
> Example 1: *Songs in Spanish for Intermediate Grades* (New York: Macmillan Publishing Company, 1991), 57.
> Example 2: Stark, op. cit.

De la Sierra Morena
page 54:
> Example 1: Spanish source unknown.
 page 55:
> Example 2: Traditional Mexican song, *Cielito Lindo*
> Example 3: Marie V. Esquibel, project coordinator, *Musica de Nuevo Mexico Para Cantar y Bailar* (Albuquerque: The University of New Mexico, n. d.)

BIBLIOGRAPHY
INTERVIEWS

Apodaca, Victor, Taos, New Mexico.
Klare, Mary Helen Fierro, Los Alamos, New Mexico.
Neri, Ofelia, Chico, California.
Perez, Anjelica, Chico, California
Trujillo, Corinne, Alcalde, New Mexico.
Trujillo, Teresa, Taos, New Mexico.
Vincent, Jenny, San Cristobal, New Mexico.

WPA Files, Archives of New Mexico, State Records Center, Santa Fe:
    Anonymous, #2.
    Armendaris, Aurelio, #28.
    Baca, Florentine, #153, February 1939.
    Berg, Manuel, #165, September 1937; #145.
    Brown, Lorin, #171; #214.
    Chapin, Genevieve, #134.
    Martinez, Aurelio, #466.
    Martinez, Louisa, #341.
    Martineez, Reyes N., #490;#466; #382; #482.
    Monreal, Cleofas, #145.
    Pacheco, Mrs. Emilio A., #165, September 1937.
    Rejada, Simeon, #153, February 1939.
    Ulibarri, Eugene F., #573.

    Also Files # 7, 9, 24, 26, 56, 148, 197, 199, 214, 222, 343, 355, 388,
    400, 402, 407, 419, 444, 458, 465, 488, 576.

WPA Files, Palace of the Governors Historical Library, Santa Fe:
    Anonymous, 5-5-49 #42.
    Batchen, Lou Sage, 5-5-47 #46, December 1940.
    Gurule, Jose and Pedro, 5-5-47 #46, December 1940.
    Gallegos, Guadalupe, 5-5-6 #13; 5-5-6 #2.
    Lynn, Bright, 5-5-6 #13; 5-5-6 #2.

NEWSPAPERS, PAMPHLETS, COLLECTIONS

Archuleta, Lisa, Berlinda Herrera, Roselia Montoya, Gloria Ortega, Julie Ann
    Pacheco, Patsy Tafoya. "Puso Uno..." El Crepusculo, Taos *News*,
    February 16, 1989.
Mondragon, Roberto. Rio Grande *Sun*, April 18, 1991; June 6, 1991.

Canciones para la Juventud de America, compilas por la Facultad de
    Ciencias y Artes Musicales de la Universidad de Chile y la
    Asociación de Educación Musical de Chile, Volume II (Washington:
    Unión Panamericana, Secretaria General, Organización de los
    Estados Americános, 1960).

Compendio de Folklore Nuevo Mejicano—Conjunto de las Tradiciones, Creencias y Costumbres Populares (Santa Fe: La Sociedad Folklorica de Santa Fe, Nuevo Mejico,n.d.).

Juegos y Juguetes de Nuevo Mexico, Hispanic Cultural Heritage Project of the Museum of New Mexico, (n.d.)

Songs in Spanish for intermediate Grades (New York: Macmillan Publishing Company, 1991).

The Oxford Dictionary of Quotations, Third Edition (Oxford, New York, Toronto, Melbourne: Oxford University Press, 1980).

Aranda, Charles, collector and translator. *Dichos: Proverbs and Sayings from the Spanish* (Santa Fe: Sunstone Press, 1975).

Brown, Lorin W., with Charles L. Briggs and Marta Weigle. *Hispano Folklife of New Mexico, The Lorin W. Brown Federal Writers Project Manuscripts* (Albuquerque: University of New Mexico Press, 1978).

Campa, Arthur L. *Hispanic Culture in the Southwest* (Norman: University of Oklahoma Press, 1979).

Carley, Isabel M., editor. *Orff Re-Echoes* (Cleveland: American Orff Schulwerk Association, 1977).

Cobos, Rubén, collector and translator. *Refranes: Southwestern Proverbs* (Santa Fe: Museum of New Mexico Press, 1985).

Cordova, Gilberto Benito. *Abiquiu and Don Cacahuate: A Folk History of a New Mexican Village* (Los Cerrillos: San Marcos Press, 1973).

Espinosa, Aurelio M. (J. Manuel Espinosa, editor). *The Folklore of Spain in the American Southwest: Traditional Spanish Folk Literature in Northern New Mexico and Southern Colorado* (Norman: University of Oklahoma Press, 1979).

Espinosa, Marie V., project coordinator. *Musica de Nuevo Mexico Para Cantar y Bailar* (Albuquerque: The University of New Mexico, n.d.).

Garcia-Matos, Manuel. *Cancionero Popular de la Provincia de Cáceres* (Barcelona: Consejo Superior de Investigaciones Cientificas Instituto Español de Musicologia, Consejería de Cultura de la Junta Regional de Extremadura,1982).

Gil Garcia, Bonifacio. *Cancionero de Extremadura,* Tomo I (Badajoz, Spain: Imprenta de la Excma. Diputación, 1961).

Gil Garcia, Bonifacio. *Cancionero de Extremadura,* TomoII (Badajoz, Spain: Imprenta de la Excma. Diputación, 1956).

Gomez-Taberna, Jose Manuel, editor. *El Folklore Español* (Madrid: Instituto Español de Antropopooogía Aplicada, 1968).

Gonzalez Barroso, Emilio. *Cancionero Popular Extremeño: Recopilación, adaptaciones, indicativo de tonalidades, transposición musical y comentarios* (Badajoz, Spain: Biblioteca Básica Extremeña, Universitas Editorial, 1985).

Gonzáles, Dolores, editor. *Canciones y Juegos de Nuevo Mexico* (Santa Fe: Museum of New Mexico Press, 1973).

Hernandez de Soto, Sergio. *Juegos infantiles de Extremadura* (Jerez de la Frontera: Editora de Extremadura, 1988).

Les, Aurora Lucero-White. *Literary Folklore of the Hispanic Southwest* (San Antonio: The Naylor Company, 1953).

Mendoza, Vicente. *Lirica Infantil de Mexico* (El Colegio de Mexico, 1951).

Palarea, Alvara Fernaud, editor. *Cuadermos de Cultura Popular: Melodias Tradicionales para Uso Escolar* (Caracas, Venezuela: Consejo Nacional de la Cultura Conac, 1988).

Posada-Charrúa, José. *Games and Songs of Mexico* (Redwood City, CA: Friedel Musikalien Haus, 1990).

Robb, John Donald. *Hispanic Folk Music of New Mexico and the Southwest: A Self Portrait of a People* (Norman: University of Oklamoma Press, 1980).

Ryan, Jim, editor. *Chiquitos: Hispanic and English Songs with Orff Instruments, Games and Dances for Pre-K through First Grade* (Leon Valley, TX: Brain Dance, Ink, 1990).

Schindler, Kurt. *Folk Musi c and Poetry of Spain and Portugal* (New York: Hispanic Institute, 1941).

Stark, Richard B., editor. *Juegos Infantiles Cantados en Nuevo Mexico* (Santa Fe: Museum of New Mexico Press, 1973).

Vizuete Carrizosa, Manuel and Juan Guteirrez Casala. *Juegos Populares Extremeños* (Salamanca, Spain: Consejeria de Education y Cultura, 1986).

Weikart, Phyllis S. *Round the Circle: Key Experiences in Movement for Children* (Ypsilanti: High/Scope Press, 1987).

West, John O. *Mexican-American Folklore:Legends, Songs, Festivals, Proverbs, Crarts, Tales of Saints, of Revolutionaries, and More* (Little Rock: August House, 1988).

Weigle, Marta and Peter White. *The Lore of New Mexico* (Albuqueruqe: University of New Mexico Press, 1990).

Weigle, Marta, editor. *Two Guadalupes: Hispanic Legends and Magic Tales from Northern New Mexico* (Santa Fe: Ancient City Press, 1987).